You Are Never Too Small To Make A Big Difference

Beth Rosenthal Davis, Ed. S., NBCT

Contributions by

Rebekah & Benjamin Davis

You Are Never Too Small To Make A Big Difference

www.teachkidskindness.com

This book is dedicated to:

Grandpa Ben & Grandma Sylvia who taught me to only see the good in people and to be kind to all I meet. My **mom** for always believing in me, no matter what I was up to and being a constant source or encouragement. My **dad** whose courage and determination taught me to be thankful for every day I wake to greet a new day.

My husband **Andy**, It has been said that being married to me is a career...I love you for standing beside me and supporting every little idea that came out of my head, no matter how ridiculous and for encouraging me to, "stop and smell the roses."

My daughter **Rebekah** for being such a kind and caring soul. Your positive attitude, wit and sense of humor always puts a smile on my face.

My son **Benjamin** for teaching me the importance of slowing down to appreciate what I have and the importance of having fun.

My best friend **Diana** for being like a sister to me, that says it all!

Drs. **Tobin, Zwibel,** & **Aptman** for making it possible for me to get a college education; it is because of you that I was able to become a teacher and touch the lives of so many lives.

Diane Baker, Roz Pass, & **Rachelle Nelson** for always having listening ears and open hearts.

Dianne & Alan Collins for you continued love, encouragement, and support. Thank you for your coaching and teaching me life lessons; anything is possible in a world of infinite possibilities.

To the special teachers in my life, from Kindergarten to Adulthood; **Pat Parham, Linda Lentin, Barbara Silver, Clemencia Waddell, Kam Patton, Ruth Alperin, Etta Gold, and Gisella Moran,** you have all been an inspiration to me. Thank you for helping to shape who I am as an educator and administrator. I model my career by your examples.

My School Family, the **Staff at Kids For Kids Academy** for your constant love, support & encouragement. Thank you for your willingness to find the gifts and talents in every child. I couldn't ask for better people to spend my days with.

To **Gabriella Miller**, a kind child who knows the importance of helping other and who is a role model inspiring those she meets with her hear of gold.

The thousands of **Kids 4 Kids Club** members for changing our community by your kind deeds and the kids at **Kids For Kids Academy** for your daily hugs and kisses that brighten my days.

The **Parents at Kids For Kids Academy** for entrusting me with your most precious gifts. If a smile is a light of friendship, you have certainly brightened my path in this world.

Foreword by Dianne Collins

Author of *Do You QuantumThink?*

New Thinking That Will Rock Your World

Every one of us is born a blessed bundle of joy with the potential to move the world with the tiniest acts of kindness and caring. The sensitive, sweet, inspired spirit of a child very naturally wants to help, to contribute, to give, to make a better world. All we require is guidance and nurturing and acknowledging of that power inherent in each one of us. In this wonderful, amazing, charming and important book, Beth Davis shows us how.

The song lyric "Teach your children well" resounds through every page as you read about children who at the youngest ages have created causes for good, have volunteered with boundless enthusiasm, have extended a helping hand and a loving heart to their fellow small-sized human beings, that each and every child may enjoy an abundant and productive, happy and healthy life. All because a parent, a teacher, a friend showed them the way.

With the storytelling ease and profound wisdom of a saint, Beth Davis becomes that friend to all of us. With childlike wonder she whisks you up, up and away on a magic carpet ride of kindness and caring through stories and experiences that will warm your heart, ignite the most elevated aspects of your soul, expand your mind—and fill you with the meaning and purpose of what life is all about—caring and sharing. All the while standing firmly on the ground of practical action, planting and sowing seeds of human potential as she has you realize how truly easy it is to make a difference.

Beth Davis puts her arm around your shoulder and guides you through conversation and story, personal experience and practical ideas for actions you can take and teach your children—advice that when taken, will quite literally change the world. These stories are not fabrications or fantasies; they are stories from real life, Beth Davis' actual experiences. Beth relates them from her heart—a heart as big as the sky—through her many roles as a teacher, a parent, a daughter, a friend to humanity and a champion for children.

You will be inspired and moved to tears. You will be called forth in your own way into action. You will know confidently how to take the hand of a child and bring out in them the inherent desire to give, ours by divine birthright. As the Torah states so eloquently, "Deeds of giving are the very foundations of the world."

We are born into the experiences and given all the talents and traits and idiosyncrasies we need to fulfill on our unique purpose. In my work, I have learned to recognize these qualities in others.

I will always remember the day I met Beth. She was just about to graduate and begin what would be become her illustrious career as an educator. Except at that time in her life, she had no idea of what was in store for her. She sat a bit timidly across the table from me in the Cuban restaurant in Miami where we met for lunch on the advice of her cousin, Andrea. Andrea somehow sensed that when I met Beth and "saw" who she was, that I would cut to the chase as they say, and, yes, make a difference in the direction that Beth would take. At that time, it appeared that Beth was about to "create" a hide-out kind of life for herself, lacking the confidence to envision something that befit her noble stature and humanitarian purpose. Her cousin was right. Through a shy demeanor, I saw a beautiful, brilliant woman who was destined for greatness. As she spoke, I was becoming frustrated that Beth didn't know her own magnificence. I have to admit, I did say a few things that shook her at her core (in a loving way of course).

As Beth always does, she rose to the occasion by taking a sharp turn and making different life choices that would alter her destiny. In her first year of teaching she was named one of the top 100 teachers in the USA by Newsweek magazine and named Rookie Teacher of the Year for the state of Florida. Her story continues with each succeeding year of major accomplishments, winning awards, teaching teachers, contributing to curricula, becoming an owner of her own preschool – and probably her most shining glory, starting the Kids 4 Kids nonprofit that teaches children they "can change the world through acts of kindness." By engaging young children in giving to their fellow youth, you nurture their natural capacity and yearning to give to others, to help one another, to be there at someone's side when needed, to brighten their day, and to know their power to transform others' lives forever by simple acts of kindness.

Beth Davis does all this, not to achieve notoriety, but with the humblest of hearts, simply to give all she can to our children and our world. Perhaps that's why Divine

Intelligence granted Beth her "original" shyness. The mission statement of her school reads: "We believe that every child has unique gifts and talents. It is our responsibility to find and nurture those gifts and talents in every child." One thing I can tell you for sure—Beth Davis is the real deal.

Now, as with anyone who has truly mastered an area of life, Beth Davis offers the priceless value of her experience to all of us in this precious gem that every parent and teacher should read together with their children. We learn together that through simple acts of kindness we transform adversities into miracles of love, of commitment and connection. By teaching our children well, we create a better world. As Beth states with genuine matter-of-fact flair, "You are never too small to make a big difference." You are never too big to make that difference either.

Introduction

When you read biographies of leaders, many of them talk about how they were shaped by their early experiences in helping others, which was something taught by their families. No matter how old your child, volunteering as a family is a great way to spend time together, while teaching values to your child and instilling a sense of community. An Independent study found that 67 percent of adults who remembered that their family volunteered when they were young said they now volunteer as adults. In contrast, only 42 percent of adults who did not remember volunteering with their family when they were young volunteer now. Studies suggest that kids are more likely to develop a strong sense of empathy when their own emotional needs are being met at home (Barnett, 1987).

This book is written as a guide for teachers and parents seeking ways to educate children at a very young age. Their acts of kindness can make a difference in the world we live inhabit. Regrettably every time you turn on the television, it seems more prevalent to hear and read about increasing incidents of children and young adults doing harm to one another and less and less recognition of children and young adults helping their community. Although not mentioned on the front page of the newspapers, there are thousands of children reaching out to help those in need, making good choices on a day-to-day basis, guiding them on a path to becoming empathetic adults.

This book not only gives practical ways to teach empathy to children, it also chronicles acts of kindness of my daughter, Rebekah Davis, from the age of 3 to 13 in an effort to show that by teaching empathy at a very young age, it becomes a lifestyle choice; one that can shape a child into becoming a good citizen in today's society. This book also shows how small groups of kids in Miami from ages 2 through 18 created a movement called **Kids 4 Kids** to help others and the impact ripple effect their work has had in South Florida. Finally, you will be inspired by how the families in one small preschool in Miami, Kids For Kids Academy, have responded time and time again to local tragedies and how they have come together as a school "family."

Take A Close Look At Yourself....What Do You See?

Before we continue, I invite you evaluate your relationship to money. If you look, you will realize how unimportant money really is and how your life will be filled with riches worth more than money itself once you realize this. Close your eyes and think for a moment, what is it that you really need to survive? Your list might include things like food, clothing, shelter, perhaps transportation, electricity, people who love you, good health, healthy family members, and good friends. Consider for a moment that if you have all that, not much else matters. Some of the happiest people are the ones who have the least.

Once you change your relationship with money, you will learn that when you help someone else, you will feel like one of the richest people on earth . There are no words to describe how blessed you will feel and how unimportant all the "stuff" becomes in your life.

Before turning the page, take a moment to evaluate your relationship with money. You will find that your relationship with money will affect your children as well as their view about the value of the dollar. I believe that there is also a direct correlation between what you feel you have or don't have and the level of service you provide in your community. Again, your level of service can either inspire or inhibit your children's commitment to serving their community.

As you think of your relationship with money, think for a moment how much money you have. Is it enough? Do you feel there is never enough? Do you aspire to have more?

If you are not sure, ask yourself the following questions: Do you live in your car, a homeless shelter, on the street, or are you blessed to live in a house or an apartment?

Do you and your children go to sleep hungry at night or are you fortunate to have access to healthy and nutritious food?

Do you, your parents or any of your children, have cancer or other life threatening illnesses, or are you and your children blessed with good health?

Have you, or anyone in your family, been victims of earthquakes, hurricanes, or tornadoes that took away all of your possessions or is your life uneventful?

After answering these questions, I hope that you find your family to be richly blessed. I think it is important to keep things in perspective and realize no matter how much or how little you have, you can always find someone who has less.

Here is where opportunity exists. Once you can get back to basics in this materialistic world we live in and realize that whatever you have is enough, you can begin to become more compassionate to the needs of others.

At my stepfather's funeral, the Cantor Rachelle Nelson, shared the thoughts of Author Davie Josephson whose insights serve to teach us how to live a life that truly matters.

> "Ready or not, some day it will all come to an end. There will be no more sunrises, no minutes, hours or days. All the things you collected, whether treasured or forgotten, will pass on to someone else. Your wealth, fame and temporal power will shrivel to irrelevance. It will not matter what you owned or what you were owed. Your grudges, resentments, frustrations, and jealousies will finally disappear.

So, too, your hopes, ambitions, plans, and to-do lists will expire. The wins and losses that once seemed so important will fade away. It won't matter where you came from, or on what side of the tracks you lived on, at the end. It won't matter whether you were beautiful or brilliant.

Even your gender and skin color will be irrelevant. So what will matter? How will the value of your days be measured? What will matter is not what you bought, but what you built; not what you got, but what you gave. What will matter is not your success, but your significance. What will matter is not what you learned, but what you taught. What will matter is every act of integrity, compassion, courage or sacrifice that enriched, empowered or encouraged others to follow your example.

What will matter is not your competence, but your character. What will matter is not how many people you knew, but how many will feel a lasting loss when you're gone. What will matter is not your memories, but the memories that live in those who loved you. What will matter is how long you will be remembered, by whom and for what.

Living a life that matters doesn't happen by accident. It's not a matter of circumstance but of choice. Choose to live a life that matters...

We make a living by what we get; we make a life by what we give."

Let's Put Things in Perspective

The little things we take for granted in our day to day life, can be life altering for others. Think for a moment about those little things that seem so insignificant to you, and how your life would be if they were suddenly taken out of your life or that of your child.

Consider this, each year on Halloween your child picks out a new costume and heads out trick or treating. Now think for a moment about the ten year old who by no choice of his own has found himself living in a homeless shelter. If it were not bad enough to live in a shelter, that innocent ten year old is told that he cannot go trick or treating. Why? First, no money for a costume. Next, most homeless shelters require that residents be checked in at a certain time of the evening to secure a bed. Lastly, most shelters are not in neighborhoods you would want your child to be walking around in.

The simple joy of a bag of candy on Halloween is taken away from homeless kids and kids living in shelters. How can you help? Gather a group of kids; ask each one to donate a bag of their favorite candy. Decorate brown bags and fill them with assorted candies and deliver them to local shelters so the kids living there can enjoy the simple pleasure of a bag of candy on Halloween. You can also ask your friends to donate their Halloween Costumes after Halloween (they are getting a new one next year anyway) and donate those costumes to kids who can't afford them. The more you can involve children in giving to others, the more empathic they become and the less they take their own things for granted.

How about your house or apartment? No matter how big or small it is, or how great the neighborhood, it is still a roof over your head. Consider for a moment the mom who lives in her car with her child and takes him each morning to McDonalds or WalMart to use the restroom to wash up. For many of these kids, the only food they get each day might be the free breakfast and lunch provided at their school or childcare center. At night their stomachs ache with hunger. Imagine for a moment, when the car they are living in gets repossessed, and the mom has no place for her child to sleep. How scary it must be for that mother and child to sleep on the street or in a public restroom. This is not an unusual situation. As a teacher, I have seen it far too many times. After reading this, I invite to you walk through the door of your home and realize just how lucky you are. Take a deep breath, look around your home and smile, knowing that you have a place to call home.

Have you ever wondered what it must be like to be a foster child? The things these children go through in an attempt to survive would turn your stomach. Unlike your child, who is tucked in his or her bed and has story time before going to sleep, these children wonder what bed they will sleep each day. As a teacher I have been fortunate to have the opportunity to become close to many foster kids. One in particular was moved so many times, that I often lost track of her. I watched this child go from one foster home to the next. With each move, the few possessions she had were moved with her in a black garbage bag. I can only imagine how humiliating it must have been for her. It sends a message to the child that they are like trash that belongs in those bags. What a blow to their self-esteem. Sometimes the clothing that followed her was not her own. I remember how she would escape the system and spend weekends with my family. We treated her like she was our own throwing her the first "real birthday party" at the age of ten.

My daughter, Rebekah, noticed on several occasions that she would wash her socks in the sink. Curiously, she inquired and learned that she only owned two pair of socks and needed to wash one pair each night and would wear the dry pair in the morning. That is when Rebekah, age 9, decided to collect new socks for foster kids. **One Sock Two Sock, Donate New Socks** became the mantra as 4,000 pairs of socks were donated to Neat Stuff, a place where foster kids can go twice a year for a few new outfits, socks and underwear.

How can you help a foster child? Donate NEW clothing to facilities that provide clothing for foster kids. New clothing is something that these kids rarely, if ever, have. While new clothes would certainly be a luxury, gently used clothing is also much needed and greatly appreciated. You can also take nice duffle bags or soft sided suitcases and donate them to foster care agencies so that, when a foster child moves, they can move their things with dignity.

As you look through your thousands of family photos, think about what it must be like to be a mom living in a shelter. Food is a necessity, photos are an expensive luxury that can be out of reach. Imagine never having photos of your child as they grew up. Simple fix....take a camera to a shelter and offer to take family portraits. Develop them and return the photos to the families. You don't need to be a professional to do this, just someone with a heart to share with others. The memories you will share with these families will warm their hearts for a lifetime.

Next time your child has his or her birthday party, hold back on the glitter and glitz. Go to a homeless shelter and throw a simple party with cake and ice cream and some gifts for the kids in the shelter celebrating their birthdays. Let your child give up one or two of their gifts for someone who has less.

For every sad story, there is an opportunity to help the sun to shine and change the life of another with very little effort.

Here is something to reflect on, author and lecturer Leo Buscaglia once talked about a contest he was asked to judge. The purpose of the contest was to find the most caring child. Here are some of the winners:

A four-year-old child, whose next door neighbor was an elderly gentleman, who had recently lost his wife. Upon seeing the man cry, the little boy went into the old Gentleman's' yard, climbed onto his lap, and just sat there. When his mother asked him what he had said to the neighbor, the little boy just said, 'Nothing, I just helped him cry.'

Teacher Debbie Moon's first graders were discussing a picture of a family. One little boy in the picture had a different hair color than the other members. One of her students suggested that he was adopted. A little girl said, "I know all about adoption, I was adopted." "What does it mean to be adopted?" asked another child. "It means", said the girl, "that you grew in your mommy's heart instead of her tummy!"

Whenever I'm disappointed with my life and things seem unfair, I stop and think about little Jamie Scott. Jamie was trying out for a part in the school play. His mother told me that he'd set his heart on being in it, though she feared he would not be chosen. On the day the parts were awarded, I went with her to collect him after school. Jamie rushed up to her, eyes shining with pride and excitement.. 'Guess what, Mom,' he shouted, and then said those words that will remain a lesson to me....'I've been chosen to clap and cheer.'

An eye witness account from New York City, on a cold day in December, some years ago: A little boy, about 10-years-old, was standing before a shoe store on the roadway, barefooted, peering through the window, and shivering with cold. A lady approached the young boy and said, 'My, but you're in such deep thought staring in that window!' 'I was asking God to give me a pair of shoes,' was the boy's reply. The lady took him by the hand, went into the store, and asked the clerk to get half a dozen pairs of socks for the boy. She then asked if he could give her a basin of water and a towel. He quickly brought them to her. She took the little fellow to the back part of the store and, removing her gloves, knelt down, washed his little feet , and dried them with the towel. By this time, the clerk had returned with the socks.. placing a pair upon the boy's feet, she purchased him a pair of shoes.. She tied up the remaining pairs of socks and gave them to him.. She patted him on the head and said, 'No doubt, you will be more comfortable now..' As she turned to go, the astonished kid caught her by the hand, and looking up into her face, with tears in his eyes, asked her. 'Are **you God's wife?'**

Examples such as these exist all around us. In her book *Do You Quantumthink,* author Dianne Collins emphasizes that our thoughts create our reality. She states that, "As you think, so you become. If you change your thoughts, you change your reality."

As you learn ways to teach your child to be empathic toward others, I invite you to change how you view your world and envision ways that you and your family can help **be** the change you wish to see.

What Does It Mean To Be Empathetic and Why It Is Important To Teach Empathy at a Young Age

Have you ever been asked to put yourself in someone else's shoes? This is an easy way to think about what it means to be empathetic. Empathy is an emotional skill that helps children to understand what others are feeling, and teaches them to treat others with kindness, compassion and love. It is empathy that encourages an individual to reach out and comfort someone else when in need. When someone falls, your empathic instinct has you putting out your hand and helping them to get up. It is also what draws you to hug and comfort someone who is crying, whether it is a child who sees an adult cry responds by saying, "Mommy, it's ok, don't cry," or an adult who comforts a child by simply saying, "Let me kiss it and make it feel better."

Have you ever seen a lost child? Your immediate instinct is to help the child find a parent. For a child, the same might be true if they find a lost pet and they instinctively try to help the lost pet find their way back to its owner. Empathy is what compels us to open a door for someone whose hands are full. It is empathy that has us comfort someone who has experienced a loss.

Empathy is an important developmental process that all children need. It is through empathy that children learn tolerance and understanding of each others' differences. An empathetic child will approach someone who looks different or has a disability and offer to help, or be their friend. Being empathetic is an important trait in order to teach positive behaviors in both children and adults. By teaching children to recognize different feelings and emotions, they can begin to understand how those feelings and emotions impact others. By learning to become empathic at a young age, children can grow to be emotionally mature adults.

Preschoolers tend to be very self-centered by nature and might not always appear to be empathetic toward others. They have to learn to take turns, for example, and learn not to push others who are in their way. The more chances young children have to learn empathy, the more empathetic they will be as they grow older.

Evidence shows that simply "going through the motions" of making a facial expression can make us experience the associated emotion and it's not "just our imagination." When researchers asked participants to imitate specific facial expressions, they have detected changes in brain activity that are characteristic of the corresponding emotions. Participants also experienced changes in heart rate, skin, and body temperature (Decety and Jackson 2004).

One way to begin teaching children about emotions is to first help them understand how to identify different emotions. For example use picture cards showing different emotions.

Lay out the emotion cards (you can order these cards from educational websites or catalogs) and ask questions like;

> Which card shows how someone feels if they lost their pet?
>
> Which card shows how someone would feel if they got a special present?
>
> Which card shows someone who is tired or worried?
>
> Which card shows someone who is sleepy?

After identifying the emotions expressed on the cards, ask the child how they are feeling, and if they have ever had such emotions. Let them describe to you when they felt that way.

You can also go through magazines and ask your child to describe how the people on the pages might be feeling by looking at the expressions on their faces. You can cut out the photos and make collages for each type of emotion. To make the activity more personal, take photos of your child displaying different emotions and put the photos in a little photo album.

What Research Shows

A report from *Independent Sector and Youth Service America* illustrates the strong impact of youth service on the giving and volunteering habits of adults. *Engaging Youth in Lifelong Service* reports that adults who engaged in volunteering in their youth give more money and volunteer more time than adults who began their philanthropy later in life.

Key findings:

- **Forty-four percent** of adults volunteer and two-thirds of these volunteers began volunteering their time when they were young.
- Adults who began volunteering as youth are **twice as likely to volunteer** as those who did not volunteer when they were younger.
- High school volunteering recently reached the **highest levels in the past 50 years.**
- Those who volunteered as youth and whose parents volunteered became the **most generous adults in giving time**.

Activities To Instill A Sense Of Empathy In Children

- School-aged children may enjoy visiting nursing home residents who may not have many guests. Contact the Recreation Director at a nearby facility to ask whether there are any residents who would enjoy the company. Playing board games together, working on puzzles or even simply chatting can brighten the day of a lonely man or woman. Kids who play musical instruments can volunteer to share their music with the elderly.

- Establish a relationship with your neighbors, bake brownies to welcome new ones

- Plant produce and donate the harvest to a local food bank.

- Plant seeds. Sell the flowers or plants and donate the proceeds to a local homeless shelters.

- Pick up litter at a park.

- Make treats or draw pictures for a local senior home.

Inspired By A Legacy

Empathy is something that is clearly instilled at a young age. Looking back, I can tell you that as a young child I was inspired to dedicate my life to serving others and to be empathic by my grandpa Ben.

Benjamin Krasnostovsky was born on May 1st, 1903 is Rochez, Ukraine. His mother was a homemaker and worked the fields and his father a farmer. Benjamin's parents both died when he was very young. His extended family was very poor. Grandpa Ben once told me that the only way he knew to be close to his parents after their death was to sleep, sometimes barefoot on their snowy graves. Sometimes when I complain about little foolish things, I think of how my grandfather felt as a child in the cold snow sleeping on top of the earth where his parents lay beneath him.

Benjamin got his lucky break in life when his cousin died. You see his uncle Frohm was due to come to America. His son died prior to departing and it was decided that Benjamin would be brought to America in place of Frohm's young son.

Upon entry to Ellis Island, Ben's name was shortened to Benjamin Krasnow. Alone and again homeless in New York, Benjamin relied on the kindness of strangers to help him on his path in life.

Although never formally educated, Benjamin Krasnow was a very successful man, one rich not in money, but in love for those around him and a passion for helping others. During his 90 year life, he had a gift store that sold China in New York, he embroidered towels and flags in a factory . He delivered meat for a butcher, learned to sew lamp shades in a tiny closet and eventually had a factory in New York. Later in life had several successful lamp stores in Miami in which carried many of the designs created by he and his loving wife of Sylvia.

Ben was kind and caring toward others whether human or animal. Some of my fondest memories were going to breakfast with him. He would always take a piece of bread from the table or crackers and break them up and wrap them in a napkin. It would drive my grandma crazy! He would walk through the parking lot and leave a trail of crumbs for whatever hungry bird or duck lived nearby. Even though, he was threatened with fines for feeding the ducks at his apartment, he never stopped. He would say, "If I don't feed them who will?" When he died at the age of 90, he left behind a wife of over 60 years, 3 daughters, 9 grandchildren, and many great grandchildren. I model my life after my grandpa Ben. He was my hero.

"Grandpa Ben" passed on a passion for helping others. Were it not for strangers who helped him along the way in life, he would not have been so successful. I choose to reach out and help others to make their lives just a little better. In the movie "Pay It Forward", (someone stops to help a complete stranger during a crisis and instructs the person as follows) the protagonist says, "Rather than pay me back, pay it forward and help someone else." I choose to live my life "Paying it forward".

Growing up and working in Miami, a melting pot of economic and cultural diversity was the perfect backdrop for community involvement. In 1989 at the age of 21, I became a teacher. Before me in the classroom were young children, blank slates waiting to be inspired. As a teacher, I had the opportunity not only to teach the three R's, but to help influence young minds and hearts. I was energized, enthusiastic, and idealistic. The more I spent with my students on community projects, the more I realized that children were hungry to help others. All they lacked was the opportunity. Small class projects turned to into school-wide projects, eventually reaching county-wide. The energy and enthusiasm seemed contagious.

"Unless someone like you cares a whole awful lot, nothing is going to get better, it's not."

Dr. Suess

Activities To Instill A Sense Of Empathy In Children

- Pick up trash on the school grounds.

- Develop and maintain a recycling program at school.

- Collect food, warm clothing, toys, or personal care items for the needy. Deliver to shelters. Remember, shelters are in need of supplies all year long!

- Hold a Teddy Bear and Friends (Stuffed Animals) Drive. Donate the collected animals to a Homeless Shelter for new arrivals.

- Encourage friends to donate gently used books to families in shelters, low income preschools or hospitals.

- Put together a care-package for teen moms.

It All Began With Peanut Butter

I will never forget the first project. After a lesson with my students on how lucky they were to live in a home, with food on the table, a roof over their heads and clothes to wear, I told them that not all children living in Miami were as fortunate. The group of 4th graders learned about the homeless living virtually in their backyards.

Through brainstorming, the class decided to decorate brown bags with beautiful pictures and fill the bags with love in the form of a homemade peanut butter and jelly sandwich, juice, fruit, and homemade cookies. As a class, they knew they could do more to help in their own community so they began an afterschool club called "Youth Ending Hunger". The children in the "Club" learned that over 60,000 people a day die of chronic persistent hunger. They held a penny drive and poured 60,000 pennies on the playground pavilion and provided a visual representation of hunger in America. The money was donated to The Hunger Project.

In the years to come the compassionate children who were my students and others like them inspired school wide feeding programs. Although sometimes dangerous, I still remember delivering over 10,000 meals bagged with love to the homeless in the streets of Miami over the next decade. My mom would worry that I would be hurt on the streets of Miami. I was worried that, in my grandpa Ben's words, "If you don't reach out a hand to feed them, who would?" Each meal I handed out my window and each bag left beside a sleeping homeless person on the street represented a young child who shared their heart with someone else. Not only did the homeless get a meal to nourish their bodies, but the beautiful drawings on the brown bags brought joy to their souls.

In my heart, my hope was that these lessons of sharing and caring would follow these children throughout their lives and that they would continue to be caring citizens. Years later, I would be blessed to have opportunities for my own children to deliver these food bags. I believe that the opportunities my own children had, to contribute to the homeless, helped to instill a sense of empathy in them. A foundation was laid for their future, so they would continue to open their hearts to others.

Disappointment Become An Opportunity

In 1995, then in my third school as a teacher, I was faced with a terrible disappointment. Just a week prior to The 6th Annual School Wide Bagged Meal Project which had produced thousands of bagged meals over the years, a mysterious airborne illness spread throughout the school where I was teaching. The Center For Disease Control (CDC) in Atlanta was called in and it was determined that hundreds of children were becoming sick from what is now known as the Norwak Virus.

I was saddened to hear that the preparation of food by children was no longer permitted. I was devastated thinking of how I could continue to share the message of helping thy neighbor now that there would be no more brown bags to fill. No more brown bags decorated with artwork of innocent loving children filled with food to nourish the soul of someone who hungered for food and love. Little did I know that there were bigger opportunities waiting around the corner for my students.

Then 9 months pregnant with my first child, I was instructed to go on maternity leave, as it was not healthy to remain in the infected school. On December

5th, 1996, I gave birth to Rebekah Evelyn at 8:15 am. She was an empty slate just like the many students I had taught and grown to love. In my arms I held an opportunity to pass on the lessons of caring and sharing. I will never forget nursing her one night during her first month of life. Looking down at her face I was taken back to my childhood. We were not a wealthy family by any means, but I vividly remembered the first day of school each year. Every year my mother made sure I had a brand new pack of crayons. Not the Crayola 64 pack with the built in sharpener. Not even the 24 pack. It was a simple box of 16 perfectly sharpened Crayola crayons.

As I closed my eyes, I remembered how they smelled, how they looked, and the special place they occupied in my desk at school. Looking into Rebekah's eyes, I knew that no matter what, she would always start school with those new pointy brilliant colored crayons; not the 64 pack with the sharpener...the 16 or 24 packs would be just fine!

As I held her close, I cried thinking of all the children I had taught over the years who had their hearts broken on the first day of school. That magical moment for most when the teacher tells the class to put away their school supplies and the room is filled with excitement as the children organize their supplies in their desks. On each first day of school I would see the pain in the eyes of those children who had no school supplies as they tried to disappear or even slide down in their chairs so as not to be seen as poor; perhaps a foster child, a migrant child, or a homeless child.

On that dreadful day each year those children were judged and labeled, not as children with the potential to be anything, young and innocent minds with incredible promise. Young children can be cruel without meaning to be. Without the interception of a teacher, those children could be friendless after such an experience. I have heard horror stories of high school kids too ashamed to confess that they were homeless.

How uncaring teachers would be when they found out kids had no school supplies. I knew homeless kids in high school that would rather take a detention for coming to school without the proper school supplies than let on that they didn't have a place to live and that their parents had no money for school supplies.

My heart broke thinking of the pain in that youth's decision.... the thought of taking a punishment for something they had no control over, to be spared the humiliation of letting people know you were poor.

In that moment, with Rebekah held to my breast, I promised myself I would spare those children that humiliation on the first day of school. It was on that night in January, 1997 as I put Rebekah to sleep that Kids 4 Kids, Inc. was born.

Activities To Instill A Sense Of Empathy In Children

- Donate video tapes, DVD's, or unused video games to local pediatric hospitals or shelters.

- Collect unused make-up, perfume and other cosmetics for a center for abused women.

- Hold a drive to collect baby items and donate to teen moms in alternative schools.

- Make center pieces, holiday cards, birthday cards, and notes for assisted living facilities, children hospital wards, or meals on wheels.

- Make Halloween bags of candy for homeless kids Be sure all candy is individually wrapped and avoid candy with peanuts.

The Kids 4 Kids Club

Kids 4 Kids was created to inspire a small group of students to learn to help others. Little did I know the impact such a group of children would have. What began with 25 kids in my own class, grew over the next 10 years to include over 300 members a year completing projects, at their meetings twice a month before school. The kids in the club became energized and there was no holding them back. Small projects soon took on a life of their own and became school-wide projects. I believe that young children want to help others and all they need is a vehicle. Kids 4 Kids became the vehicle that started these 7 to 11 year olds on a path of service. Not because it was a graduation requirement, they did it because it made their hearts feel good to care about someone outside their circle.

Twice a month they arrived at our school at 7:30 a.m., an hour before school started to make their mark on the world, one small project at a time. They made birthday cards for homeless kids,

Valentines for kids in foster care, get-well cards for kids in hospitals and collected toiletries and bagged them with welcome cards to welcome homeless families as they arrived at shelters.

They decorated and filled thousands of bags with candy so that homeless kids could enjoy their own bag of candy on Halloween. Care packages were made for troops serving our country complete with inspirational cards and little love notes. Food drives for Thanksgiving and toy drives for the December holidays also provided opportunities to share with others. There were projects to prepare teen moms for their new bundles of joy, as kids in the club collected new baby items and filled baskets with love.

One project that reached the community was the Kindness Cards Project. A longtime dream of CBS 4, Neighbors 4 Neighbors Director, Lynne Cameron this became a reality with the help of the Kids 4 Kids Club.

The children drew beautiful pictures on one side of an index sized card, while the other side had a special message in Spanish and English;

"You just performed a random act of kindness. I noticed and wanted to thank you for doing so. Please accept this card as a token of thanks. When you see someone else doing something kind for someone else, please pass this card along to them."

Neighbors 4 Neighbors produced the cards by the thousands. And their distribution inspired many others to begin performing kind acts for others. Lynne's great idea combined with the passion of the children who created the cards, started a wave of caring throughout the community. This appreciation of everyday individuals making a difference, inspiring others to do the same with the simple concept of "Pay It Forward."... If you haven't seen the movie *Pay It Forward*, put this book down and go rent it. It will change your life!

Ten years later, "out of the blue," I was given one of the cards designed by a Kids 4 Kids Club member from a complete stranger.   By then, I was the owner of a preschool. I provided free tuition to a widowed single mom. She gave me a kindness card in return. When I looked at the card, I was moved and felt a special warmth in my heart, knowing that it had come full circle. I remembered the child who made that card, knowing she had to be 20 years old.   I wondered how her involvement in Kids 4 Kids helped to shape her life. Not only did I experience the joy of getting the card but the joy of knowing the child who made this card I was given. I wondered if the lessons she learned when she participated in the Kindness Card project had made an impact in her life.

These young children were also inspired to action by disasters around them. Kids 4 Kids jumped

into action by holding book recycling drives. After Hurricanes, the entire school "family" joined in and collected gently used books that they were no longer reading or had outgrown. Within a week, 95,000 books flooded the school and were shipped off to those schools affected by the disasters. The impact of this literacy project has been replicated over the years and those recipients have donated to disadvantaged children in their own neighborhoods. We all hoped that by owning their own books we could instill a love of reading.

When we saw how easy it was to have people "recycle" books they no longer wanted, the kids in the club held more "Book Recycling Drives." I still smile at the thought of the bus load of books that arrived at West Homestead Elementary and how the children in Kids 4 Kids spent the morning laying out the books. This was their own makeshift book store. I remember the tears of joy that rolled down my cheek as I watched those caring children escort the less fortunate one by one as their own personal shopper. They were helping their new friends to choose books to start their own home learning libraries.

Both the giver and the recipient had a life altering experience on that day. The recipients saw the books as gifts more precious than gold or silver. Those books would help them on their way to reading: what could

be a greater gift? The giver felt joy in knowing the impact they had made on the life of another child. I invited the kids in the club to go home that night, to re-read their favorite book and think about their new friends, snuggled up in their bed enjoying the gift of literacy that they had helped provide.

Activities To Instill A Sense Of Empathy In Children

- Have a drive to collect NEW socks and underwear for foster kids.

- Donate used eye glasses to an organization or place that recycles them for the needy.

- Make a holiday basket for someone in need.

- Collect gently used clothes and donate them for a dress-up area at a daycare or family shelter.

Say Cheese!

They say that a picture is worth a thousand words. Perhaps the most moving of all Kids 4 Kids sponsored "projects" was the Homeless Family Portrait Project. As a mom, I have had the good fortune to pour over innumerable photos of my children. I look back and remember their every stage of development. Their birth, to their first steps, their faces covered with spaghetti and I take myself back to each developmental milestone. I consider myself very fortunate. I thought about homeless moms who not only are without a place to live, but lack something like a camera and wondered how hard it must be to only have pictures in your mind of your child growing up.

It was then that I partnered with Larry Mayo, then an Area Manager for a school photo company. Capturing childhood memories was his business. His company took the photos at my school. After speaking to him, he came to understand how devastating it would be for a mom who never had a photo memory of her children. After all, he was in the business of making memories. Without hesitation, he committed his staff and the company resources to the project. Each year for ten years, his staff would show up at homeless shelters at both ends of the city and allow families living in the shelter to pose for family portraits. Tears would fill my eyes to see the families, moms with kids, grandparents and their grandchildren, single dads, complete families, young mothers with babies waiting for pictures. They all loved their children as much as I loved mine. They sat proudly wearing their best church clothing, some borrowed, as they stepped up for their turn. For some, this would be the first photo ever taken with their families.

I looked at them and imagined how they might feel years later looking at the photos and remembering the hard time in their lives and this special photo. How proud they could be to know that they persevered the struggle. Hundreds of photos were taken each year and portrait packages delivered just in time for Thanksgiving. What a gift to be thankful for. Unfortunately, after a long ride of over ten years and thousands of families photographed, Larry retired and the company no longer offered the program.

Although I was saddened to have lost the project, I am comforted thinking of all those it affected. I hope that in years to come when those homeless families are once again on their feet, look and remember how others opened their hearts to them when they were going through that difficult time. My hope is that those families will reflect on their photographic memories and one day too, "Pay It Forward!"

In the years that followed, other photographers have embraced this project on a smaller scale. Do you have a camera? Perhaps you can volunteer to take photos for homeless families. Something so simple can leave footprints in the hearts of many. They say a picture is worth a thousand words. It is sad to think that many disadvantaged people only have the memories in their mind of their children during their precious stages of development.

The Signature Project: The Kids 4 Kids Fill A Backpack Campaign

"Branding" of a product is very important to its success. This was also true for The Kids 4 Kids project. In its infancy, I went around looking for any donation I could find. How lucky we were the local television station, CBS 4, provided pencils for the backpacks we hoped to fill. At the time we were the program Kids For Kids. After sharing my vision with Lynne Cameron at CBS 4 Neighbors 4 Neighbors, she suggested changing the name to Kids 4 Kids, perhaps the television station could support it.

Over the next ten years, the charity, the television station and their charitable arm, Neighbors 4 Neighbors, had a wonderful partnership. They called on the kids in the club for projects and we enjoyed media exposure facilitating recognition in the community. The two, Kids 4 Kids & Neighbors 4 Neighbors were often perceived as being one in the same. Neither one seemed to care since the reward was mutual.

The kids' enthusiasm was contagious and during the first year of the club, the Fill-A-Backpack Campaign was born. The goal of the campaign was to fill new backpacks with school supplies for 500 homeless children living in shelters and attending  public schools in Miami-Dade and Broward County. We wanted to make the life of a child in need a little brighter. Students in the club, as well as other students in the school and community, became so inspired in making a difference for other kids that, at the end of the first annual campaign, 1,000 backpacks were collected, filled with school supplies, and delivered to homeless, abused, migrant, and foster children. In our second year, the club entered a National Grant Contest and was recognized by Northern Life Insurance claiming its third prize in a national competition that attracted thousands of educators. Larry Stein, their regional sales manager, flew to Miami from Atlanta with a larger than life, 5 foot check made out to Kids 4 Kids for a whopping $12,000. That money launched Kids 4 Kids, a 501©3 not for profit organization.

The contribution of Kids 4 Kids, Inc. to the South Florida community grew with each passing year. In our second year, we filled and distributed 1,500 backpacks. The third year, 3,000 backpacks were collected. Over the next three years, 4,000 backpacks were delivered annually. In August 2002, and 2003 they delivered 6,000 backpacks to school children in need and in desperate situations, to homeless, abused, migrant, and hospital homebound kids. Each year the goal increased and the project grew. From 1996 to 2011, Kids 4 Kids volunteers have brought joy to over 90,000 children who could hold their heads up high as they began school prepared for success just like their more fortunate peers.

An inspiring aspect of this is that as, kids left the club to go on to other schools, many returned each year to take part in the backpack campaign. It is humbling to see the commitment of these children and how participating in this program has brought them to a place of service to others.

My favorite time of the year is not my birthday or Chanukkah, it is to this day the two weeks before the school year begins.

It is then that we spend a week with hundreds of volunteers ages 5 and up unpacking boxes and filling thousands of backpacks with school supplies. The packing process has been fine-tuned over the years. Before backpacks can be packed, boxes piled sky high had to be unpacked. Children young and old stand among stacks of notebook paper and supplies, sometimes reaching over 8 feet high, filling a school cafeteria. In the days that follow, this well maintained

machine of volunteers, fill bags assembly line style. When the packing is complete, they are loaded and sent to the receiving agencies. One year, we had over 76 agencies waiting to serve. This including homeless shelters, low income schools, foster homes, Department of Corrections, hospitals, and other groups serving children in need.

Although the kids enjoyed packing, the real joy came in the deliveries. Early in the morning on a Saturday, youth volunteers, their families and returning older kids line up their cars in a caravan. Backpacks are loaded into cars by age. Mickey Mouse, Spiderman, Princesses and other juvenile backpacks are in one car sorted by boys and girls. Volunteers load bags for older  kids in the other cars and books and other goodies in other cars. When the cars have been loaded, the caravan moves off through the streets of Miami. Twenty or more cars begin their pilgrimage to migrant camps and homeless shelters. When we arrive and line up the cars, we are greeted by hundreds of children, many who have been waiting in line for hours in the sweltering Florida summer sun for the first glimpse of what has been prepared just for them.

One by one we introduced a volunteer to a child whose life may forever be changed by these interactions: The volunteers' feel such reward that they return year after year to experience this wonderful exchange. The volunteer is given specific instructions not to pick out the backpack for the children, the child has the choice. For many of these children, this is the first time they have ever received a new backpack and for many it is as close as they have ever gotten to "shopping" for their school supplies.

It is a privilege for me to introduce each child to their volunteer and let the volunteer know what grade the child will be attending. First I crouch down to be at eye level with the child. I look into their eyes and try to connect to each child. After asking their name, I take their hand in mine and introduce them to their personal shopper. The two leave holding hands and walk toward the car of their choice. I take a snapshot in my mind. What a beautiful sight to see! Two hearts become one as they journey to choose their backpacks. One child happy to help, the other thrilled that someone cared enough to come that day. As they walk off, they find, a Princess backpack for the little girl going into kindergarten, Spiderman for the second grade boy, a blue Jansport for the high school boy and a red one for the middle school girl. Most think they are getting just an empty backpack and they are just thrilled that someone thought of them. Watching them peek inside and seeing the joy on their faces when they realize the bag is filled with supplies is beyond explanation. They know they now have the tools to help them to be successful. Their "labels" of poor, migrant child disappear; they are now a child filled with promise!

One memory that I will always hold dear is that of blonde little 7 year old Emily, when we pulled the caravan of cars up to the shelter where she was living, she came out of her unit barefooted, and ran to the car; you could tell that she gets few visits there. When she heard that the volunteers would have stickers ready for the children, she went running to her mom, ponytails bouncing up and down yelling, "Mommy, we are going to get a sticker." The thought of getting a sticker was enough to throw her into excitement. This wasn't a Nintendo or even a baby doll. It was just a sticker, imagine what must have been going through her head when she saw cars and vans filled with mountains full of beautiful NEW backpacks, new books, instead of used hand me downs.

As I walked her along the row of cars, she stopped dead in her tracks at the "girlie" car. Her beautiful chestnut colored eyes grew large at the sight of the pink Barbie backpack. I put it on her shoulders and adjusted the straps. She smiled so big, I could see the spaces between her missing teeth. Her thanks and hugs brought tears to my eyes at the thought of how happy she was for school to begin. That year we carefully tucked post cards in every backpack hoping to hear from the kids. Days later, I received a post card from the mom of the little child who picked out the Barbie Backpack. It said…

"Dear Kids 4 Kids. Thank you for makeing my doter so happy. She sleeped with that Barbie backpack on her back last nite thinking of skool starting."

Another postcard we received from a high school child read, *"Thank you for my new backpack. I was tired of carrying my school supplies in a grocery bag. One day I hope to help someone like you kind folks helped me. I will do good in school and make your volunteers proud."* It was then that I realized that we were like the strangers that helped my grandpa Ben when he was alone in the world, just what I always wanted to be.

Here are excerpts from many other "satisfied customers",
all in their own words.

'Thank you I loved your gift. You really helped my mom out. We really appreshiate what you do. Because when you don't have a lot, you are thankfull for geting stuff that you can't get on your own. God Bless You." Monique grade 5

"Oh thank you so much. It was really sweet of you to think of a stanger. I really like my new backpack and when I make some money one day, I will do the same for someone else. Thanks again and God Bless You All." Novella grade 10

"I would like to thank Kids 4 Kids for the backpack and all the supplies. I needed them badly for my first year in High School. I will study HARD. Thank you so much!" Jessica grade 9

"I was ashamed to be a senior in high school and carry my books in a Publix grocery bag. Now I have a beautiful backpack thanks to you guys. You are really special." Elizabeth grade 12

"My dad works hard to support me and my four brothers, but there was no money left for school supplies. Thank you for thinking of us when nobody else did. I will treasure my backpack always." Jeron grade 5

"When our house burned down, all my things were burned too. I was scared to go to school. Thank you for saving the day." Melanie grade 4

'Thank you for my Barbie backpack. I slept with it on my shoulders last night. It is the first one I have ever had and it is pink. I love you." dictated to mom by Stephanie grade 3

"Dear Santa, I lost my toys and all my things when we had to move out of our house. Can you please help us? Love John" Written by a second grader who thought Santa left the backpack

"Last year I was aoneroll [honor roll] student. I like school. Thank you very much." Nick grade 4

"I want to thank all the kids who gave me the school supplies. I worried all summer that I wouldn't be able to get any. You helped me a lot, I really don't know how to thank you." *Jaime grade 11*

"Thank you for bringing me the Bat Girl Backpack. I am very happy. Now I can go to school and keep learning." *Quella grade 2*

"Thank you Kids 4 Kids if it wasent for you I would of had to use the same broken bookbag from last year. I wish you get an award for helping people like us. I hope you have a very happy year. Thanks for the suplise." *Esther grade 11*

"Thank you for taking time out of your busy schedules and summer vacation to come and bring us things and to see us." *Demetrious grade 8*

"I am very greatful and very thankful. This bookbag is big and pretty and it is big enough for all my books. Also it is good because my mom didn't have any money." *Roberto grade 4*

"Thank you for the awesome backpack. I was getting tired of carrying my books in my hands." *Jonathan grade 10*

I sleep soundly after each distribution knowing that we have spared thousands of children each year the humiliation of starting school unprepared for success.

More than a decade after starting Kids 4 Kids, I was invited to a special graduation dinner. You see, in 2009, Kids 4 Kids marked its 13th year of making back to school dreams come true for over 80,000 underprivileged kids. The children graduating were all children of migrant families. Against all odds, the kids in the room managed to complete 12 years of school. It was an honor to be in their presence. That night they acknowledged me. This group of 200 graduates, a record number for migrant kids, had received a backpack from Kids 4 Kids every year since kindergarten, this was a milestone for us all.

Speaking to the graduates that night I looked into the crowd and remembered some of their faces over the years at the migrant camps where we had hoped to have we had made a difference for those children. Standing before them, listening to their words of thanks, made me realize that indeed we had made that difference. I was touched by the comments of the graduates. One was quoted in the newspaper saying that she and her brother looked forward every year to our visits. She said how much it meant to her growing up that we believed in them when no one else did and how her success was due in part to the kindness of strangers. She was proud to share that she was accepted to Florida International University and planned to be a teacher.

Imagine opportunities that lay ahead for her classroom filled with blank canvases. Would her experiences as a recipient help her to be more empathic and instill that message in her own students? I hope one day that she passes on those lessons and that she can paint a canvas in her students to ignite them to feel the social responsibility to do good for others. Another spoke saying that although they didn't know who we were, each year, they felt that they were never forgotten at the migrant camp. One student claimed that he stayed in school against all odds because we believed in him when nobody else did.

I hope the girl who will become a teacher remembers the times that strangers believed in her as she reflects on her accomplishments, realizing the power she has to inspire others.

Activities To Instill A Sense Of Empathy In Children

- Make welcome cards to make the residents at domestic violence shelters feel welcome to their new temporary "home".

- Put together a care-package for service men/women.

- Form a litter patrol on school or park ground.

- In December, contact a tree farm or nursery about donating a Christmas tree to a needy family, shelter or nursing home, or buy a tree to donate.

- Have friends and family members collect travel sized hotel toiletries, put them in little bags with card and donate them to homeless shelters to give residents when they arrive at their "new home."

Kids 4 Kids Undergoes A Change For The Smaller

Sometimes God opens a door that you just can't walk past. If it were not for my father, I probably would still be going about my business teaching elementary kids and guiding the students in Kids 4 Kids. At dinner one night my father shared that he had always been proud of me and never knew how to show it. He asked what I would do if I won the lottery. I replied by telling him that I would buy the dwindling preschool across the street from where I taught and turn it into an amazing place for children where they could learn to make a difference for others. He sensed my excitement about the possibilities and opportunities for young children who had the opportunities that I could offer. With that, he committed to my vision and lend me the start up money and Kids For Kids Academy was born.

I felt conflicted about leaving the secure teaching position I had held for the past 17 years but was filled with excitement at the possibilities lying ahead. It only seemed appropriate to call the school Kids For Kids Academy. It would be a place to teach much younger children that they could change the world through their acts of kindness. However, two years after I left the elementary school, the club was disbanded. I found that it was very hard to export my passion and convince another teacher to take over the club. Luckily, those who learned the lessons of empathy returned each summer to pack and deliver backpacks. As alumni got older, they came to volunteer regularly at the Academy.

Kids For Kids Academy opened its doors in 2005. It was not surprising how easy it was to teach acts of kindness to very young children. The mission statement of the school was "We believe that every child has unique gifts and talents. It is our responsibility to find and nurture those gifts." It was an approach that staff embraced whole heartedly.

Young children have the gift of empathy and we gave them opportunities to share their hearts with others. When a child participated in a project and shared their heart with someone else, their name was placed on a heart on the graph of giving.

Some projects included food drives for needy families, Halloween bags for homeless kids, new socks for foster kids, "adopting" inner city preschools for the holidays, and even participating in the Relay for Life where our school raised $2,000 for cancer research. We also raised money for two families in our school who were effected by Muscular Dystrophy. Families at the school love the fact that we fostered an environment where kids can learn to care for others at a young age. In just 7 years, our enrollment climbed from 47 children to 200. We believe that in addition to our unique science and literacy program, our community outreach inspired families to attend our school. I was inspired by several families in the school who encouraged me to write this book as a guide to raising empathetic children.

Activities to instill a sense of empathy in children

- Hold a food drive to help keep food bank shelves well stocked.

- Donate gift cards for teens in foster care, they are the most forgotten.

- Ask your friends to donate $5 grocery gift cards each time they go to the grocery store for their family. Put all the cards together and provide a complete Thanksgiving meal for a family who may be down on their luck.

- Offer to walk a neighbors pet if they are feeling ill.

- Make cookies for a new family in the neighborhood.

- Make gifts for soldier serving our country.

Attracting Disasters

Reflecting on the first 7 years that Kids For Kids Academy has been open, I can't help but notice how many times bad things have happened to good and innocent people. I say this because with each new school year, it seems that another tragedy affects families at our school. In looking back, I can see that although bad things happened to good people, those events impacted the families at our school in such a way that they were propelled into action. Similar to the way Kids 4 Kids Club members were called to action, Kids 4 Kids was just a vehicle for them to use.

I started realizing that as long as I showed willingness to serve others and the ability to open my heart to others, disasters kept showing up on my doorstep. Looking back, I see that although something horrible happened each of the first 7 years the school was open, each event provided an opportunity for the families and staff at the school to be called to action. They were given the opportunity to step forward and change the life of someone else. At the same time, they had the opportunity to realize how fortunate they were to not be in the position of those families in crisis. I invite you to be open to accept what comes your way and to be willing to help. Somehow, things will be put in your path and by stepping up to help, not only will you affect the lives of others, your heart will be warmed beyond belief.

Each opportunity to help others will also give you the opportunity to continue to count your blessings for what you have in your life and spend less time reflecting on the things in your life that aggravate disappoint or sadden you on a daily basis. By reaching out a hand and opening your heart, your life will be forever changed for the better. By allowing your children to see you helping someone else, it will help them to be more empathetic as well.

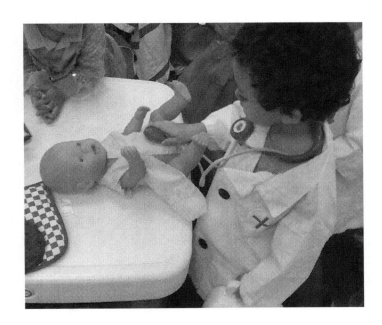

Heartbreaks Turn to Opportunities

During our first year, it was little Davie. I will never forget the phone call I got at 8:00 am on a rainy Tuesday morning in March. The call came from the office of a nearby apartment complex manager. The caller asked if 4 year old Davie attended our school. When I said yes and inquired why the caller was asking, I was told that Davie's mom had a heart attack the evening before. Apparently, a worker entered the apartment to perform routine maintenance using a master key to open the door. There he found Davie in his Kids For Kids Academy T-Shirt worn to school the day before.

Davie's mom had died from a heart attack at the dinner table the night before and Davie told the worker that he was unable to "wake her up" so he slept in his school shirt next to her body. I can't even imagine what could have been going through Davie's little head. Was he cold or hungry? Did he try and wake mommy only to find that she "slumbered on" unable to heed his cries for help?

We were called since there was no one who could identify a next of kin to take Davie. They asked me to look in his file and find an emergency contact. The only name in the file of this single mom was her mother in Naples, several hours from Miami. Not knowing the relationship, I called the person on the phone and was heartsick when I asked her relationship to Davie. When she said she was the grandmother, I felt myself break out in a sweat, the hairs on the back of my neck stood up and time seemed to stand still. It was then that I realized that I was about to tell this woman on the other end of the phone that her daughter died of a heart attack the night before and her grandson, Davie, was alone in the apartment all night with his dead mother. The elderly woman on the other end of the phone wept in disbelief.

I raced to the apartment and stayed with Davie while the ambulance took his mother away. I brought him a stuffed toy to hold. The police gave him a red balloon. What he thought would be an exciting day with the nice policeman would end up being a day that would forever change his life. I waited with Davie and the police until someone from The Department of Children and Families (DCF) arrived to take him away. Since I was not related to him, I had to let him go to be united with his elderly grandparents.

I wondered what would become of Davie. During the next week, his grandparents stayed in Davie's home while putting his mother's affairs in order. As a psychologist, my husband counseled Davie and helped the grandparents to realize that the best life for Davie would be with an aunt. Davie had met her only once; She lived in Spain with her husband and two children. Within weeks, this little English speaking 4 year old was swept away to Spain to begin a new life. The families and the staff of the school donated $1,200 to help Davie and his transition.

Although we never wish for bad things to happen, when they do, it is comforting to know the tremendous impact a group of individuals can make to help someone survive a crisis.

Activities To Instill A Sense Of Empathy In Children

- Write a compliment and give it so someone who did something nice.

- Have your child pick out school supplies for someone who needs them at back to school time.

- Have an UN-birthday party at a shelter and bring ice cream, cake and a gift for each child there.

- Cut down on holiday gift giving and give a gift to someone who really needs one.

- Keep non-perishable food in the car at all times in case you see someone who is hungry.

- Make holiday decorations and take them to a shelter.

The Strength Of Family

The second year it was little Frank's mom. I will never forget the day I met Frank. He was brought to school by his aunt and uncle. Their own kids attended our school in years past. Frank and his mom went to live with them when her cancer became very aggressive. It was then that the two families became one. Frank loved his mom dearly. It was heartbreaking to watch as she slipped away from him. Emily was a woman with the strength of steel. She loved to bring Frank to school and attend whatever events she could with him, even though her pain was obvious. Emily would have to leave for weeks at a time to get treatments in another state.

Everyone, including Frank's Abuelita (grandmother), knew that Emily's cancer was terminal and she would one day leave her little Frank. Although we were all sad when Emily left this world, the family had comfort in knowing that her suffering was over and she was in God's presence. Once again, out of tragedy came humanity. The school community came forward to offer support to little Frank. He was blessed a hundred times over, despite losing the one thing he held most dear.

You see, during Emily's last months, her brother and his wife, along with their three girls, took Frank and Emily in and he became a part of their family. A family deeply committed to God, they loved Frank as if he was their own. It was only natural after Emily's death that Frank remain with them. It was a joy to watch Frank over the next year as he grew into a beautiful young boy. I grew very close to the entire family including Margaret, Frank's grandma. She taught my daughter and me how to knit caps for cancer patients. This was something she did while Emily was hospitalized.

This family helped show everyone that in the words of the Beetles, "All you need is love....Love is all you need."

Activities To Instill A Sense Of Empathy In Children

- Donate diapers to low income childcare centers, homeless or domestic violence shelters.

- Hold a penny drive. People don't mind getting rid of them and they add up.

- Keep an empty 5 gallon water bottle in your house. Drop your pocket change in it at the end of the day. When it is full have your family decide how to spend the money.

- Have a bake sale or set up a lemonade stand and donate the money to charity.

- Grow your hair and your child's too. When it reaches a really long length, cut off 11 inches and send it to Locks Of Love to have a wig made for a sick child who has no hair. Your hair will grow back, theirs may not.

Grandma Is Gone

The following year, something horrific happened and again tragedy turned to opportunity for the families at our school. I will never forget the night that little 3 year old Oscar's mom came late to pick him up. She was hysterical, beyond consolation. She wept as she told me that her mom, who lived in a townhouse across the street from them was missing. Her mom was not ill and was in a good mental state. She had arrived from Cuba months earlier and would go back and forth to her job each day using public transportation.

Oscar's mom continued to weep as she explained the mystery surrounding her mom's disappearance. She said that the front door of her mom's house was unlocked and her mom's keys and purse remained on the kitchen table. We speculated...did she wander off, was she kidnapped? There were no clues, this mystery made no sense. Oscar's mom spent the next few days riding the public busses all over Miami showing her mom's photo, hoping that someone, anyone would recognize her. I connected the family with my friends at CBS 4 and, before we knew it, her photo and story was all over the news. After weeks of hunting for her mom, there was finally a break in the case.

Oscar's grandma was found dead in the bushes outside Miami Metro Zoo. It still has not been determined whether she wandered off and had a heart attack or whether she was murdered. It was unclear how long she laid in the brush just a half mile from her home and what killed her. In the end, it appeared she was mauled by wild dogs.

If this tragedy was not horrible enough, the family had no money to pay for a funeral. Once again, tragedy turned to opportunity. The opportunity for the families at Kids For Kids Academy and the community to once again come together. There are good and caring people in this world. Within a week, enough money had been generated to pay for Abuelita's cremation and a religious service giving the family a chance to say goodbye to their loved one.

Activities To Instill A Sense Of Empathy In Children

- After your child's birthday party ask them to choose one of the gifts to give to someone else. Birthday and holiday time is also a great time to have your child choose toys to give away to someone else to make room for their new ones.

- Cut back on holiday spending. Sometimes less is more. In some countries, kids get pennies in their shoes.

- Donate clothing when no longer used. Donate unused toys too.

- Special Olympics- Volunteer at the next Special Olympics event in your area. specialolympics.org.

- Help the animals. Children love animals, so why not use this interest to help out at your local Humane Society by donating your time or supplies (pet food, old blankets, etc.).

Heartache in Haiti Finds a Family in Country Walk

The world watched in horror on January, 2010, as an earthquake in Haiti claimed the lives of thousands of innocent people. A tragedy so far away found our little school propelled into action. Compassionate families here wanted to help families there. Within days of the disaster, families from Haiti sought refuge in Miami.

A vacancy in the shopping center where our school is located provided a place for a makeshift little store. Families from the school began bringing in items new and gently used. Within a few short days, the 1200 square foot space was filled with clothing, shoes, toiletries, diapers, formula, toys, and food. We got a call from the United Way and learned of a plane filled with babies, orphaned by the killer earthquake due to arrive soon. They were to be taken to a makeshift orphanage, but one problem.....they had no car seats to transport them from the airport.

With one e-mail, the parents from Kids for Kids Academy again opened their hearts. Within a few days, our little store had 14 car seats donated to assist in the transport. The empathy shown by the parents at the school was amazing. The orphans were picked up and taken to a military base; the donors went home and hugged their children feeling blessed that they were safe in their arms.

Word began to spread to newly arriving families from Haiti of our makeshift store and they began to arrive hoping to start rebuilding their lives... no money, no appointment needed. As fast as the supply shop emptied, kids from local schools and churches got on the bandwagon and made donations to help fill it again.

There were two families who found their way to us that touched our hearts and soon became members of our school family. Both families were in Haiti and watched in horror as their homes fell down on top of them. Lucky to get out alive, they told stories of family members who perished. I was particularly moved to hear of a young boy who went to school and never returned home. The thought of the anguish his family had to endure waiting, praying, and hoping for his safe return was overwhelming. I can't even fathom the anguish that mother felt. I could not continue living if my child went to school and never came home. One of the moms was pregnant and although she endured hell on Eearth, she was blessed just a month later with the birth of her sweet baby boy.

We invited both families to begin rebuilding their lives at our school, to become a member of our extended school family. We knew we couldn't afford to offer full scholarships to the four children, but also knew that we couldn't turn them away, not as long as our own two children were safe at home.

We held a "Hearts for Haiti" weekend. Parents came to a charity dinner and they shared an afternoon with their kids at a carnival in the school parking lot. Families from the school had a chance to share with someone else and also had a chance to look into their own lives and realize that they were blessed. The fundraising weekend collected nearly $7,000; enough to pay for one of the children to attend for a year. By that time, we grew to love both families and were inspired by their will to heal. All four children were enrolled in the school.

The kids adjusted well. Luckily one of our teachers was from France and was able to help with the language barrier by speaking to the children in French. One family left our school after a year to move to Canada. The second family remained, and years later, has become one of the most loved families at the school. I get joy on a daily basis seeing mom and watching her three beautiful children as they grow and thrive. Years later, their dad remains in Haiti trying to rebuild the country. Mom enters our school every day with a smile on her face and love in her heart. Their resilience is a testament to the strength of young children. They are able to move forward in the face of disaster. I am also witness to the difference committed mothers can make in their children's lives.

Activities To Instill A Sense Of Empathy In Children

- Plan a charity carnival for your backyard complete with carnival games, refreshments, and prizes. Afterwards, donate all the proceeds to your favorite charity. Invite friends from your neighborhood, place of worship, and your children's classes by printing up flyers (indicating which charity will benefit). Charge a set fee for entrance. You can set up a ticket booth and give guests tickets to use for games and refreshments.

- **Support a Local United Way Charity.** Use the United Way website to find a volunteer opportunity in your neighborhood.

- For many kids, Halloween is one of the most fun holidays of the year. What could be better than getting dressed up in a crazy costume and going from door to door to get tons of free candy? Your family can have fun on Halloween and at the same time help children and families in need Donating your candy, collecting change for UNICEF.

- Hold a car wash, donate the proceeds to a charity of your choice.

Miracles For Madison

All of the tragedies we faced in our first five years were horrible, but nothing could have prepared our school for what happened on September 9th, 2010. I will never forget where  I was when I got the call. I was observing Rosh Hashanah and on the way to the cemetery to pay respect to my grandparents. Almost simultaneously as I passed Baptist Hospital, I got a call from the school telling me that 1 ½ year old baby Madison was in that very hospital. She was taken in for a suspected ear infection. It ended up being a brain tumor. The final diagnosis was yet to be determined.

My first reaction was to burst out in tears. You see, just the day before, the gifted teachers of her class called Madison's mom, Susie, to let her know that Madison was not "quite right". Susie picked up Madison and was frustrated and flustered. Just the day before, Madison went to the doctor who said that she was not sick, but did have 4 teeth coming in. That said, there was nothing anyone could say to explain this.

I made a U-turn and arrived at the hospital where little Madison was getting a CAT Scan. Susie's mom wept as she explained that they found a large tumor on the baby's brain and she would soon be whisked off to surgery. All we could do was go home, hold our children tight, and pray for our little angel. That evening, Madison underwent brain surgery. The surgeons tried to remove the entire tumor, but 10% of it was badly calcified. Each time they touched the remaining 10%, baby Maddie's heart would stop. It was then that they decided to stop the surgery. After the 7 hour surgery, the pathology was sent away while everyone waited and prayed for a miracle.

Another MRI revealed that the calcified part of the tumor was keeping the fluid around the brain from draining. A stint was put in so that fluid could be drained from the head. The next day, doctors clamped the drainage tube and the family prayed that it would drain on its own so that they could begin to address the tumor. They needed to determine if it was cancer and if so, what type?

If the fluid did not drain, a tube could be run to the stomach so that the fluid could drain and be absorbed into the body, but if it was cancerous, the drain in the stomach would no longer be an option as the cancer would spread through the body.

Days later it was determined that Maddie had a very rare and aggressive form of cancer called AT/RT (Atypical Teratoid/Rhabdoid Tumor). This type of cancer is a very rare, fast-growing malignant tumor of the brain and spinal cord. It usually occurs in children younger than three years of age, although it can occur in older children and adults. About half of these tumors form in the cerebellum or brain stem. The cerebellum is the part of the brain that controls movement, balance, and posture. The brain stem controls breathing, heart rate, and the nerves and muscles used in seeing, hearing, walking, talking, and eating. AT/RT may also be found in other parts of the central nervous system (brain and spinal cord).

The moment we heard it was cancer, we were propelled into action. We were determined to do whatever could be done to support this horrific period in the family's life. The first thing was to give the family an outlet to share Madison's progress. We wanted a way for members of the community to send written prayers and good wishes to the family and a way to donate much needed. I contacted our talented web designer, Ray. Without hesitation, he created a page for Madison on our school website.

The months that followed were filled with ups and downs. Everyone at the school was talking about how they could support this family in its darkest hour. The next day, along with two parents from the school and three teachers from Felix Varela Sr. High (where Madison's mom, Susie, was a teacher), we gathered at a nearby restaurant. We formed a committee called **Miracles For Madison**. A talented young artist designed a logo and shirts were made. The committee grew to involve people throughout the community planning events for Madison.

There were ice cream nights. Restaurants donated money from sales to the family, concerts, garage sales, movie screenings, spaghetti dinners, raffles, and a huge event that took place on Madison's second birthday. We held a walkathon/carnival/ music fest.

Although Madison was enduring two months of Proton Beam Radiation and countless chemo treatments, we celebrated her birthday in style. There was a light at the end of the tunnel. In April 2011, just seven months after being told she only had a 10% chance of survival, Maddie beat the odds. No signs of cancer were found on the MRI!!! We all rejoiced and felt wonderful knowing that the community came together to raised nearly $80,000 to help heal this child.

Just weeks later, rejoicing turned to heartache as the family realized that Madison was losing her sight. A new MRI confirmed that just a few treatments shy of the completion of her protocol, new tumors were causing Madison to lose her sight. Despite the earth shattering news that the cancer came back, Madison continued her fight against the wicked cancer monster. Unable to walk, talk, or see, she remains an inspiration to everyone who hears her story.

In January 2012, Miracles For Madison held a third Birthday Party with all the trimmings; six inflatable rides, ponies, clowns, game booths manned by local high school kids and tons of food. These were ALL DONATED! Madison showed up before the event started (to avoid contact with the crowd) and had a chance to explore the party and the animals in the petting zoo. Susie, Madison's mom, joked that next year when Madison is well, she will be disappointed at a normal party with just one bounce house minus the ponies, clowns, and the trimmings. Sounded great to me! At the end of the day, the community came out and donated $6,515 to be used for Madison's speech and physical therapy treatments.

Madison was being raised as a blind child and continues to be a source of inspiration to everyone who hears her story and sees her beautiful face. As of the initial writing of this book, Madison, age 3 ½, had completed her second 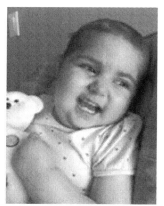 round of cancer treatments and is tumor free. The family rejoiced when Madison started making sounds for the first time in two years. "Vavavavavavavava" were the most beautiful sounds that the Schafer Family had ever heard. This miracle for Madison could have been the beginning of her ability to speak. Think of the sounds of beautiful and courageous Madison, "Vavavavavavavava" as you celebrate the tiny miracles in your day today. The staff at Kids For Kids Academy and the families whose children attend the school kept the faith that Madison would return to the school and be a part of the Pre-Kindergarten program when she turns four. To show their conviction for Maddie, the entire staff wears purple Miracles For Madison shirts every Friday.

In May 2012, the rug was pulled out from under us all. What we all expected to be a routine 3 month follow up MRI showed that Madison's frail little body was filled with cancer cells. The community cried, not understanding how this could have happened. The cries of joy just 3 months earlier turned to cries of sorrow when we heard that the doctors would give little Madison Star only months to live.

On Friday July 13th, Madison left this world peacefully surrounded by her parents in their Miami home. At her funeral, hundreds gathered to pay tribute to the little girl who lived her life like a rock star. She touched thousands during her brief time on this planet. Her courage, strength, and determination have become a benchmark for how other live their lives.

Months later, I went through a McDonalds drive through and the voice on the speaker asked, "Would you like to donate a dollar to the Rondald McDonald House? Without hesitation, I said, "Yes." The voice over the speaker replied, "REALLY!" I sensed that he was not used to getting people to say yes to this simple request. I did without a second thought.

I remembered how Susie and Madison's two month stay at the Ronald McDonald house during her radiation treatments were filled with love and hope. When I got to the window to pay, the boy handed me a star shaped piece of paper for my donation. I wrote "For Madison Star" on it and handed it back to the boy. He looked at the star and said, "Did you know Madison?" When I said yes, tears filled his eyes and he said, "Did you know she died?" I said yes and he and I wept as he handed me my order.

He explained that he was a student at Varela Sr. High, the school where Madison's mom Susie worked as a math teacher. As I help up the line of cars he told me that the school raised money for her treatment and how she inspired him. Out of her suffering, so many children and adults learned the meaning of service to others and that their acts of kindness can help their neighbor.

Like everyone else, I wake up from time-to-time and find my day to be not as fabulous as it could be. The unexpected is always there. Sometimes I catch myself complaining about the little things in life. When I do that I always come back to Madison and her story. Madison and the strength of her family is always a source of inspiration for me. No matter what is going on in my life, I say to myself, "At least my children are healthy and I don't have to go through the hell that the Schafer's have endured the past two years and may endure in years to come. Thank you Madison for helping me put my life in perspective everyday. You and your family are my role models and heroes.

Activities to instill a sense of empathy in children

- Hold a community garage sale and raise money for charity.

- Hold a bake sale and donate the proceeds to charity.

- Donate used board games, video games, movies and other toys your kids no longer use to local shelters.

- Collect recipes from friends and family members and make a cookbook. Sell it to raise money for charity.

- Encourage families at your child's school to make pans of pasta and salad. Sell tickets to a spaghetti dinner and donate the money to charity.

- Go to garage sales. Buy **new** toys and clothing and donate them to kids who need them. You can use the money from your family charity box to buy the goods. "Garage sailing" is a fun thing to do together.

- Donate the books your child has outgrown.

I Continue To Learn Life Lessons

Although I am not a superstitious person, Friday the 13th of April, 2012 served as another wakeup call to me and my school community. I am a person that just cannot sit still, someone who always feels that enough is not enough. I regularly work 12 hour days in pursuit of excellence in my career. Stopping to smell the roses, was not a phrase in my vocabulary. That day started out as usual at my preschool. There was the hustle and bustle of the end of the week. There were little frustrations over being short staffed, and being tired. There were knee hugs and kisses from little angels at the preschool, and conversations with parents at the school. I even had a conversation with a parent at the school that encouraged me to pick up this book again and continue writing, something that I had no time for over the past six months. Near the end of the day, I remember thinking, that I would spend the weekend resting. Resting is not easy for me. I would spend some time working on my book.

Then the walls came crashing in. I got a call from a parent at the school asking if we had a family at the school with the last name of Camacho. I told her little

Bella was in our three year old class and her brother was in our school last year and is now in kindergarten. While on the phone with her I checked the computer and realized that Bella was not in school that day. In the moments that followed, my heart missed many beats. The caller told me that there was a horrible car accident and she saw a photo of Bella with the Easter Bunny at our school on the news. It was in the debris field.

Apparently Bella's dad was driving his two older daughters to school and their car was struck by a drunk driver going 90 miles an hour in the bus lane. In a second, their lives changed forever. In the back seat was Bella's 13 year old sister Kaely, in the front, her 16 year old sister, Breann. The news footage showed the car and there was no longer a back seat. Kaely, died leaving a family to mourn and the community left asking WHY? "Why do bad things happen to good people?" Why do people make stupid decisions like drinking and driving? There are no reasonable answers to these questions. Both the lives of those who knew and loved Kaely and the families who came to help, will never be the same.

At midnight, I spoke with Ray, our web designer. Within minutes a link to donate for funeral expenses was on our website. Within hours, families from the school started donating money. As the funeral approached, in two short days, the families at the Academy donated $1,500 to the Camacho Family. Although the money could never ease their suffering, they gained comfort in knowing that their family was in the hearts and prayers of so many strangers. The weekend for many was introspective, looking at our lives, hugging our children and wondering why. As I write this I am numb, unable to fathom the enormity of this tragedy. Another opportunity for me to count my blessings. Maybe this time to stop and smell the roses in my own garden.

Activities To Instill A Sense Of Empathy In Children

- Older kids can tutor low income children needing help in school.

- Have a movie night, charge admission and provide snacks. Donate the money to charity.

- Older children who babysit can offer to babysit for free for single parents who need a night out.

- Volunteer to set up a gift wrap station at holiday time. Gift wrap at no charge and encourage customers to give a donation.

- Donate Halloween candy. Excess candy can be donated to Meals on Wheels, nursing or veterans' homes, shelters or agencies that work with children (such as foster care, group, or transition homes). Treats like these are especially appreciated on Veterans' Day, Thanksgiving and other holiday parties.

- Make Get Well Cards for people in hospitals.

A Perspective of Giving Through the Eyes of a Child

Rebekah's Point Of View Written At Age 13

What Is A Mitzvah And

What Is The Importance Of Giving?

Not everyone in the world has the same luxuries that many people are privileged to have. I say this because some people are not fortunate enough to have food on the table three times a day, electricity, a stable shelter to live in, or even clothing to wear; some people wear the same clothing every day. I was taught at a young age to help others so that others can share in the simple day-to-day luxuries that I am fortunate enough to have. In Hebrew, a mitzvah translated to mean, a good deed. Simple mitzvot could be holding a door open for someone who needs help, sharing food with someone who is hungry, or even just being there to listen when someone has a problem. If nobody ever helped others by performing mitzvot, the world would be really sad. There would always be someone who would have nothing and be in need of help and there would be nobody to help them.

I am a Mitzvah Maker, here is my story. It all started in 1999 when I was 3 years old. I was helping my mom with her project, Kids 4 Kids. This is an organization that teaches kids that they can change the world by helping others. Since 1996, they have donated 80,000 new backpacks filled with school supplies and 90,000 new books to homeless, abused, migrant, foster, and low

income families. Since the beginning, I have volunteered for Kids 4 Kids.

This photo shows my first memory of helping others. At age 3, I gave juice and candy to every kid who stood in line for a backpack at homeless shelters and migrant camps. As I got older I got to help fill the backpacks and take the kids by the hand and escort them to pick out their very own backpack. (2002-2008)

As member of Kids 4 Kids, I attended meetings at my school twice a month, completing a new project each time. Some projects included filling and decorating bags for homeless kids so they would have something sweet to eat on Halloween. We also made pins for soldiers serving our country, Valentines bags for foster kids, collected travel sized toiletries for homeless

families, gift drives for the holidays, turkey baskets for Thanksgiving, and much more (www.kids4kids.org).

After the attacks of 9/11, when I was 4 years old in preschool, I made flag pins with safety pins and beads. I sold each pin for a dollar and raised enough money to buy blankets for 28 kids living in a shelter. I also gave them my stuffed toys.

In 2002 & 2006, I cut about 11 inches of my hair and gave it to an organization known as Locks of Love. They made the hair that I donated into wigs for someone unfortunate enough to lose their hair from chemotherapy or something like it. I was happy to give this little part of myself to someone else, no matter how hard it was. I knew that I would grow more and hopefully, always will. I was so happy that I was able to give someone my hair. I kept trying to imagine some girl, any girl, with no hair

walking into a classroom and being stared and pointed at... being the butt of jokes, by the others in the room who honestly didn't know what she was going through. With my wig, perhaps she will be able to walk into the room with her head held high, looking just like everyone else and having a faint sense of normality. With that, it was easy to part with my hair.

When I was in 2nd grade in 2004, I wrote a small book telling about how as a young child I did mitzvot for others, and sold it for $5. Using the proceeds of the sale to help a family have a brighter holiday season. For the holidays, I had adopted a family who was barely making it financially. I used the money to buy presents for the two children and a little something for the parents. I collected over $200. I still remember how the little girl was practically bouncing off the walls when I walked in with all those toys. There was enough stuff to fill up the whole dining room table at my house; we still needed to stack some and even put some on the floor.

During the years 2006-2009 I started a project called "Project New Sock." Here's why. A foster child is a kid  who does not live with their birth parents. Sometimes they are moved from foster home to foster home. Often when they moved to a new foster home, the few things they owned sometimes don't move with them. Most of them do not have their own things so they rely on donations or used toys and clothing. I had a friend named Lovely who was a foster child. She would visit our family and we would do things together. One day when I went to visit her in the hospital when she was sick, she wasn't in her bed. Instead she was in the bathroom washing her socks in the sink. Her foster parents didn't have a lot of money so they kept the money for food. Since they didn't have a lot of money they only bought her a few outfits and 2 pairs of socks. She would wear one pair one day, wash it in the sink, and then wear her other pair while the wet ones dried during the day. Through Project New Sock, I collected socks and inspired others to do the same. When all was done, over 3,000 packages of socks were donated to Neat Stuff

(www.neatstuffhelpskids.org), an organization allowing foster kids to "shop" their warehouse for two free new outfits twice a year.

When I turned 12, in December 2008, it was time for me to think of a special project to do as part of my 2009

Bat-Mitzvah. My parents own a preschool. In 2008, a little four year old boy named Frank lost his mom to Cancer. His grandma would spend her spare time knitting hats for people with cancer. She showed my mom and I how to make the hats, and that is where it  all began. We started making caps for kids with cancer. What started as a small project quickly took on a life of its own. As friends and family members started to see my progress, they thought it was a great idea and they too began making caps. My grandma Reva went crazy knitting cap after cap until her fingers were sore.

I however had a different purpose in mind. In 2005, doctors found out that my Grandpa Richard's sore throat was really stage 4 cancer which is the last stage. Doctors doubted his chance for survival. He endured a year of weekly chemotherapy and six weeks of radiation. Through his wonderful doctors and positive attitude, he is cancer free today. More recently in August of 2009, we found out my Grandma Pat was diagnosed with cancer. She however was not as fortunate as Grandpa Richard. She died just 14 days after diagnosis. I knit these caps for kids with cancer in honor of Grandpa Richard and in memory of Grandma Pat.

To make an even bigger impact giving others a chance to help someone else, we launched a website; www.capsforacure.org. Not only will the caps go to kids with cancer, individuals can make a donation to cancer research. Their name were placed on a tag on the caps. That way, kids with cancer will not only feel cared about when they wear the cap, they will know that money has been raised for cancer research. In one short year, over 200 caps were given to children with cancer and over $2000 was raised for The American

Cancer Society.

Rebekah,

I cannot begin to tell you how proud I am of you. I love you and admire your kindness and sensitivity. You are a beautiful young woman.

Love, Mom

Benjamin At Age 10

No matter how many times people tell you, don't not compare your children, it seems impossible. Unlike Rebekah, it was harder at first to get Ben into the spirit of giving. Ben, a brilliant child, loved his Legos, building, playing on the computer and watching TV. Much of the time, he was self absorbed in being a ten year old boy, bothered about having to take time away from his interests to help others. We continued to expose Ben to volunteering and one day it clicked.

On one of our visits, to pass out meals to the homeless, in Miami, Ben was taken aback by a man in a dumpster. At first he wondered how anyone would go in a dumpster, let alone, eat food from one. When we explained to him that the man was hungry and hoped to find food of any kind there, he began to realize how important the bags of food he was delivering were. After he gained an understanding of how desperate the man in the dumpster was, Ben jumped out of the car and walked toward him. He ran toward the shirtless and dirty man, waving the bag in the air, started yelling, "Mister, I have a bag of food for you!" The man was happy to see Ben and the bag of food. From then on,

Ben had a greater understanding of what it meant to someone else.

As time went on, Ben became more conscious of other poor and homeless people on the streets. Each week, on the way to Sunday school, he would see the same man in a wheelchair, with his cat strapped to the back of it, begging for money for food. Each week, Ben made sure we took some food to give the man; he started noticing other homeless people. They were like the man in the wheelchair.

One weekend in April, a simple inquiry turned into Ben's project to help others. After spending the night with his grandparents, he got in the car with a rubber band ball which amazed him. We both wondered what was in the middle and how many rubber bands covered it. Quickly he began taking the ball apart and counting the rubber bands until he counted all 300. He was excited to find a little rubber ball inside. His mind began to race. "I could make these and sell them and keep the money to buy legos." His eyes lit up at the thought of all the money he could make.

I reminded Ben that as long as he lived in our house, he would always have enough and this could be a great way to raise money to help someone less fortunate. We brainstormed the who, the what, and the how and found ourselves on a search to find colored rubber bands. I told him I would buy the materials, but he would have to write the plan and do the execution. The $1.50 it would cost me in materials for each ball Ben would make, was nothing compared to the lesson it would teach him on his path to learning empathy and the realization that the world did not revolve around his wants. Below is what Ben wrote in the planning of his rubber band ball project.

Ben's Story

"My name is Benjamin and it just breaks my heart to see the lonely man in the wheelchair with his starving cat starving every Sunday on my way to Sunday school. Every week we keep food in our car in case we see him. I can tell every time we give him food. It is mostly things he does not like, but he shows his appreciation by smiling and saying thank you anyway. Think about how you would feel if you had to eat your food out of a dumpster. There are some people I have met that can tell you the answer. I'll never forget the day that I met a man getting his food out of a dumpster. I met him while passing out sandwiches to the hungry and poor people in Miami. I felt very good that his rummaging through the dumpster ended as he began his rummaging through the bag I gave him containing sandwiches, drinks, cookies and other goodies he devoured.

I got to thinking...I am a very picky eater and if I were to be living on the street, I would go hungry because of this. Most of the time, nobody gives the people without food the food that they really like. So now I have decided to sell something I could make; rubber band balls that I could sell for $5.00. Since everyone uses rubber bands they could buy something that could help them and as an added bonus, all of the money would go to buy fast food gift cards. Homeless and hungry people could choose the food they like.

I think if they knew all people who helped them in this terrible time, they would be very grateful of the givers' generosity. I sold my rubber band balls with the following slogan: "Each time I sell one rubber band ball, I can pass out a $5 fast food gift card which they can purchase any food item they want instead of what other people want to give. Each time you use a rubber band on this special ball, remember you helped someone have a special meal that they truly enjoyed."

Ben made the first ball and I bought it right away. He made me take him right to McDonalds to buy the first gift card. It was Saturday. He knew exactly who he  wanted to give the first card to. The next morning on the way to Sunday school, Ben filled out the card to the man who inspired his idea and hoped he would see him. He wrote in the gift card holder, "I bought this for you, Ben." As we came over the overpass and inched near the highway, Ben spotted the man in the wheelchair. He opened his window and motioned for the man to come to his side of the car. The man did. Ben handed him the card and watched with joy as the man read the card and smiled. That morning, there were three warmed hearts; Ben's, mine, and the homeless man in the wheelchair with the cat nestled in the cat carrier strapped to the back of his chair. Ben said that next time, we should bring some food for his cat, too.

Later that afternoon, Ben had a chance to meet with the director of his Sunday School. He shared his idea and said he was starting his Bar Mitzvah project 3 years early. I was so proud. As he explained it, Joy, the director was in awe of the idea... the inspiration, and the realization that Ben was following in his sister's footsteps. She told Ben she thought it was a great idea and bought the only ball he had on the spot. Ben was elated to hear that she wanted to order 20 rubber band balls to give her teachers as end of the year gifts. She told Ben that it was an excellent project on many levels. He could make the product, it would make so many people happy. Everyone uses rubber bands.

Ben ran out of the meeting, grabbed my phone and called his dad. He told him that he had an order for 20 rubberband balls and that would be $100. He could buy 20 giftcards and make 20 hungry people happy. And then the production began!

Although Ben's excitement for the rubber band ball project was short lived, he did raise $300 that was used to buy Burger King Cards, kept in the car for times when we saw someone hungry on the streets of Miami. Ben had the experience of finding a solution to a problem that could help someone else. I see glimpses of his humanity in the things he says and some of his actions. Although he loves getting a warm loaf of Cuban bread on the way to Sunday school, he also loves sharing the loaf with the homeless man on the way to Temple. Each Sunday, Ben enjoys eating half of the loaf and carefully folds the bag over to save the rest for someone else. We are both happy when we see the man with the cat under the overpass. Happy that he can enjoy some warm bread and a smile. Happy to hear him say, "God Bless You."

Ben,

You are turning into a fine young man. The thing I love most about you is your kind heart.

I Love You, Mom

There Are Angels Among Us Disguised as Children

 On January 13, 2003, a precious little girl entered the world. When her parents looked into her eyes they knew she was filled with promise, but I am sure they didn't realize that she was destined to inspire the world through her acts of kindness and generosity. As she grew, Bri, as she would come to be known, set an example at a very young age proving my point... **you are never too small to make a big difference.**

As she got older, her parents taught her to be kind to others and instilled in her the Jewish value of *Tzedekah*; giving charitably. She donated her hair to Locks Of Love at the age of 8 so that a child stricken by illness and lost their hair could have the joy of a full head of hair. As she grew older, she also gathered toys in toy drives many times and delivered them with her parents to needy kids at hospitals and homeless centers. Her random acts of kindness helped to lift the spirits of those who were less fortunate. Gabriella often put the needs of others before her own.

Bri makes sure that she always has *Tzedekah* (money for the poor) to donate at Sunday school each week. She also loves to send happy cards to sick friends to cheer them up. Gabriella is a really good friend; she is loyal and sticks by her friends through thick and thin.

In November 2012, Bri began getting headaches. Doctor visits and tests confirmed that she had a walnut-sized, inoperable tumor on her brain. Many kids would have just thrown their arms up and felt sorry for themself. Not Bri. She accepted the situation and became determined to remain positive and, through this horrible ordeal, help others. You see, after being told that she qualified for a trip to Paris through The Make A Wish Foundation, she wanted to do something to give back to the Foundation and help other kids.

She learned that Macy's agreed to donate $1 for every letter to Santa dropped off at their stores, up to a million bucks! Faster than you could say cancer, Bri began her campaign to personally collect 10,000 letters so she could be part of generating $10,000 to help Make A Wish make more wishes for kids like herself. What makes this story even more inspiring is that Gabriella's family is Jewish and does not even celebrate Christmas. She put her own beliefs aside and decided to use Santa letters as a way to help others. In doing so, she gave everyone who heard her story the chance to put religion aside and embrace the true meaning of the holiday season. She showed young and old that wishes can come true if you only believe in miracles and the goodness in each person.

Word of 9-year-old Gabriella Miller's efforts to collect 10,000 letters addressed to Santa Claus spread faster than the man in red can make his rounds on Christmas Eve. What started as an email spread from Gabriella's school to local newspapers and within 24 hours became a national news story prompting children from 1 to 92 to rummage for crayons and pen their own holiday wish lists.

I have to admit, I was also caught up in the efforts. Raised Jewish myself, I never wrote a letter to Santa in my life, but I too came to realize that this was much bigger than a Christmas story; it was about the spirit of giving and giving others the chance to impact the lives of their neighbors. It was a chance for each person to reach into their hearts and help someone else. I invited families at our preschool and teachers I knew to join in and help spread the holiday cheer and help Gabriella to meet her goal.

In two short weeks nearly 5,000 letters poured into our school and my inbox was filled with letters from adults writing to Santa begging for Gabriella's good health. I must admit that I did read many of the letters. After Bri's story and request for everyone to help, I was not surprised that the letters I read did not ask for toys and electronics. The letters asked for Santa to find a cure for cancer, to end suffering, help the poor, stop wars and to bring peace on Earth. Most importantly letter writers were willing to give up all their gifts if "Santa" would make Gabriella well again. I am confident that so many wishes, so many prayers for hope and health will certainly "wish" Bri's cancer away.

The outpouring of love from Gabriella's school, temple and community became a source of strength to her whole family. Her parents were overwhelmed by the generosity of their friends and neighbors. By late in the first week, almost every regional news outlet and several national outlets, including MSNBC's Today Show, contacted the Miller family with requests to share Gabriella's story. And by the end of the week, Gabriella was swimming in letters from as far away as Poland and South Africa.

To help the effort, Bri organized Dear Santa parties, filling every seat inside Loudoun Country Day School's gym as kids and their parents munched on cookies and scribbled Christmas wish lists. Gabriella taught us that kindness has no religious boundaries.

This nice Jewish Girl could care less about Christmas, but certainly knows how to propel others into action. The Hebrew word *Mitzvah* means "acts of kindness." Bri is a "*Mitvahmaker*" in every sense of the word! Just like the Santa letters, Bri sees beating her brain tumor as just another goal to reach. When she was diagnosed, her doctor told her the tumor was the size of a walnut sitting in the back of her brain. So that evening she and her father bought a bag of walnuts and spent Thanksgiving break with hammers in hand smashing the nuts.

Bri is very smart. Despite daily radiation treatments, she has still managed to attend school and even get A's. She loves to dance, plays the  flute, joined the drama club at school and participates in plays. She teaches her little brother how to work the computer. (He adores her, even when they fight.) Bri is a real leader in every sense of the word. Her insights are that of someone far beyond her years. She wanted to teach the kids in her 4th grade about what is happening to her so that they wouldn't be afraid. So her parents, a social worker from the hospital and Bri organized an assembly for all the 4th graders, teachers and parents. She brought a model brain and a walnut to show the kids what had happened to her face which was drooping on one side because of the tumor pushing on nerves. She and her parents assured the children that Gabriella was NOT contagious and they did not have to be afraid to touch her.

Gabriella answered questions like: Does radiation hurt? How did she know she had a tumor? What is an MRI? What does the medicine taste like? She answered all the questions herself. Then her parents broke out a bag of walnuts and told the kids to come up and smash them (with mallets and frying pans) just like the radiation is smashing her tumor to dust! The kids began feeling more comfortable around her and began to understand what she was going through. Bri taught her friends something that she knows well: how to be empathetic toward others. What a great gift she has given them through her struggles. Her friends carry her book bag when she is tired. They remind her to drink all day from her water bottle. They use hand sanitizer and Lysol in their classroom so she doesn't catch colds. They are making her feel special and loved.

Word of Bri's Santa letter wish went viral. The campaign to deliver 10,000 letters to Macy's ended just a few short weeks after it began with the 240,983 letters!

Macy's was so inspired by the size of Bri's heart, drive and determination that they committed to donate an additional $25,000 past their $1,000,000 commitment to The Make A Wish Foundation. That extra $25,000 will made it  possible for 2 or 3 more special children to have his or her wishes granted as a gift from Gabriella, the Wish Maker. What a tremendous accomplishment! On December 23, 2012, crowds filled the mall to see the little girl with a big heart prove time and again that **you are never too small to make a big difference.**

I've never met Gabriela, but her determination and smile is like a light of sunshine that brightens the path of everyone who hears her story. Bri, your heart is made of gold and knows no boundaries. I join the millions who have heard your story in thinking only happy thoughts for your complete recovery. When I put my head on the pillow each night I will pray that your recovery be quick and easy. I know that you will grow up and continue to do great things. My guess is that you will become a teacher. You are already teaching so many about the power of positive thinking and that kindness is the way to live our daily lives. Keep up the great work Bri...You Rock!

*Excerpts taken from Leesburg Today article by **Danielle Nadler** and information gathered from Grandma Beverly*

Beth Rosenthal Davis

Activities To Instill A Sense Of Empathy In Children

- Save coupons and give them to people who need them.

- Knit hats for people with cancer. If you don't know how to knit, you can find an easy knitting loom at the local craft store.

- Read to kids or do art projects at a shelter.

- Cut back on birthday gifts that your children don't need. Get them a few things and ask some (or all) guests to bring a gift for an underprivileged child or ask them to make a donation to charity.

- Serve a meal at a homeless shelter.

- Write letters or draw pictures to service men/women. Fill shoe boxes with candy and snacks to send to the troops.

- Volunteer to take family photos at a homeless shelter. Print the photos and give them to the families. Many of them may have NO photos of their children.

Total Family Involvement Is Key

When looking for ways to volunteer, think of things you can do as a family. Invite other families to come along; caring can be contagious! Involve your children in the decision making process. When the ideas come from your children, they take on a greater meaning for the child. Start small; Rome was not built in a day. Even the smallest project can change the life of the person who benefits from your kindness.

When you discuss projects with your children, sometimes, the simpler the project, the better. Think of something small that they might take for granted like getting a toy in a Happy Meal. That Happy Meal toy will eventually be lost or forgotten. On the other hand, it might be more than a homeless child might have at a given time. If you have young children, why not make a box for Happy Meal Toys when they are no longer used. They can be sold by your child at their next garage sale and the money be given to charity.

How about having your child share their birthday, Christmas, Chanukkah, Kwanza or other holidays with someone else? Explain that they will get one less gift for the holiday and instead let them go to the store and pick out a gift for a less fortunate child. Explain the concept to them. There are other children who have less. Let the child help wrap the gift they can imagine the joy as it is unwrapped.

Ways To Start Young Children On A

Path To Learning Empathy

The best way to introduce children to community service is to start at home. Dr. Kalman Heller, a psychologist in Massachusetts says, "Young children have a natural tendency to care about others. The process of putting that care into action really starts within one's own family, as children become conscious of the needs of their parents and siblings."

It is also important to begin by teaching children to be sensitive toward others. Simple examples could be to understand when mom and dad have a bad day at work, when a sibling is sick or when a younger brother or sister is in need of some quiet time taking a nap. Other examples include sharing toys with friends or even just taking turns. Teach children to also share opportunities to "go first" even if it is just in playing a game or waiting in line. This helps to teach children to be fair to others. Being fair is one way to begin teaching empathy to children.

"Community involvement is so much easier if it evolves as a natural process of family growth and values," Dr. Heller suggests. "Create experiences together. Before sitting down to a big Thanksgiving meal at home, serve food to the homeless at a downtown shelter. It's a dramatic, effective way to foster the development of an attitude of concern and caring."

Think about the size of the project as well as the time commitment. Start small so that you don't get overwhelmed. You might start out with something you can do as a family, once a month, then every other week, or even weekly. The project may be interesting and encourage your child's participation.

With our own children, we began with the giving of allowance. As soon as our kids could understand that four quarters made a dollar (around age five), they began getting an allowance. The reason we did this was so that they could understand that they got a dollar for allowance, they had to put $0.25 into the Tzedakah (Hebrew word for Charity) box. As their allowance increased, so did the amount that went into the Charity box. At age six, our daughter and son got $1.00 ($0.25 for the charity box), age eight $2.00 ($0.50 for the charity box), at age nine $3.00 ($0.75 for the charity box), at age eleven $4.00 ($1.00 for the charity box), and at age twelve $5.00 ($1.25 for the charity box).

From time to time, they would come up with projects about how to use the money. Sometimes the money was used to buy gifts for children who might have none at the holiday time. Letting the kids count the money and pick out the gifts makes it even more special. Sometimes we use the money to buy food to fill bags they decorated, holding their homemade peanut butter sandwiches, cookies, juice, and fruit. Other times the money went to buy $0.49 McDonald's hamburgers; after all, as my kids pointed out, homeless people get tired of peanut butter! I will never forget the first time we took our son Benjamin to deliver bagged meals that he and Rebekah had put together.

As we continued driving, Rebekah got out of the car several times and gently left bags next to sleeping homeless people feeling comforted that they would be joyful when they woke up to a free meal. She knew that when they woke they would smile, knowing that someone cared about them. The meals went quickly and the biggest upset for Ben was when the food ran out. He saw a woman, clearly homeless and perhaps schizophrenic, talking to herself near Mc Donald's. Ben was so upset that we were out of bags that he made us drive through the McDonalds and get her a burger, fries and a drink too!

From that day on, both our kids became more conscious of the poor living in our community. Each time we cross the overpass on our way to US1 towards the Temple, there is always someone begging for food. The kids always want to give them something. Whenever possible, we keep nonperishable food in the car in case we see someone who looks hungry.

On another occasion, I stopped with Rebekah and Ben at the local 7 Eleven store for a Slurpee. I saw a man with a crutch and a hospital bracelet begging for money. Reluctant to give him money, I asked if he wanted a hot dog and a drink; more than I would have given him in cash. The man was elated. I went in and had Rebekah make an extra Slurpee for the man and proceeded to get him a hot dog. After paying, I told the man at the register that the man outside would be coming in to prepare the hot dog I had paid for. While I was paying, Ben invited the man in to dress his hot dog. As we pulled away, the homeless man said, "God bless you" and both kids could not stop watching the man eat his lunch.

Ben commented that the man seemed happy and had a big smile on his face. The memory of that smile was worth millions. We did feel blessed by God to have been able to help. Who would have known the impact a Slurpee and a hot dog could have on all of us. It is not the size of the project, but the impact it has.

Become The Change You Wish To See In The World

Sometimes it's hard to understand why horrible things happen in our world. With each tragedy I hear about, I question my faith and am just left to wonder why. Why do people die in car accidents, fires, hurricanes, tornadoes? What is the purpose of cancer and other diseases? Why do children get sick or die before their parents? Why are some people hungry and homeless while others who work just as hard have food and shelter? We can choose to feel bad or choose to use unfortunate events as opportunities to make a difference. When you hear of bad things that happen to innocent and good people, think of a way, no matter how small, you can contribute to helping the individual. Feed the hungry, volunteer at a hospital, donate your unwanted things to someone who has less.

I was heartbroken when my dad was diagnosed with stage four throat cancer. Although it is something I would not wish upon anyone, that horrible year in my dad's life gave me an opportunity to change mine. Before his cancer, I was someone who would never leave the office. Despite having an amazing top notch staff, I hated to give up control of running the operation.

My dad's cancer gave me the opportunity to be with him once a week while he was going through treatments.

Against all odds he beat cancer.

I am inspired every time I see him. His illness was a wakeup call that gave me a second chance to be a better daughter. Now years later and cancer free, lunch each week finds us at Ruby Tuesday sitting in our special booth. I look forward to the hour I spend with him each week catching up on what is going on in each other's world.

Each time sad situations cross my path I am reminded of his words to me, "Every day you wake up and put two feet on the ground, you are doing better than most." I hear these words like a mantra.

Dad, thank you for making it all so clear to me. I can choose to wake up each day and complain about the things that I don't have, the things that go wrong, or the horrible things that go on in our world, or I can realize that each day is a gift and tomorrow is not a guarantee. You have taught me a valuable life lesson. Each day I wake up and put two feet on the ground, I am doing better than most.

Take a moment and think about who inspires you. Is there a baby Madison or someone else who has overcome adversity? In troubled times, sometimes it is hard to see the forest through the trees. It is hard to see the sunshine during a storm. Remember that no matter how bad your situation is, there is always someone who deals with their own major problem. Next time you kiss your healthy child or a loved one goodnight, realize how lucky you are for having them in your life.

I invite you as you close the last page in this book, to start a new chapter in your life. Be someone who lives a life that matters. Find problems and injustices and set out to make the world a better place. Pass this message on to your children, your friends, and anyone who will listen. Be the change you wish to see in the world. Be the light of sunshine for those going through a rainstorm. I firmly believe that if we teach our children well, and lead by example, we can change the world one good deed at a time. Let your smile be the light of sunshine that brightens someone else's path in this world.

You are never too small or too big difference...you are never too big either.

"Never underestimate the power of a small group of committed people to change the world. In fact it is the only thing that ever has." **Margaret Mead**

Non-Profit Organization Founded By Children

A Place to Call Home

http://aplace2callhome.tripod.com/homeless

Teenager Kristen Thomas of Sterling, CO started A Place to Call Home after she was touched by the plight of the homeless she saw on a trip to Denver with her Dad. She and her friends Jenna and Danielle collect donations of toys, toiletries, baby food, and bibles that they then put together as care packages to distribute among the homeless in the Denver area.

Alex's Lemonade Stand:

www.alexslemonade.org

Alexandra "Alex" Scott was the 4 year-old founder of Alex's Lemonade Stand for Pediatric Cancer Research. Two days before her first birthday she was diagnosed with cancer. At the age of four, Alex decided to do something to make that cure more likely. She opened her first lemonade stand in July of 2000 with the idea of donating the proceeds to "her hospital." Each year since, Alex held an annual lemonade stand in her front yard. On August 1, 2004, Alex died peacefully at the age of 8. As word has spread, donations have poured in from around the world, and Alex's Lemonade Stand has already raised over $5 million for pediatric cancer research.

Becca's Closet

www.beccascloset.org

"Little things can make a big difference..." This was the phrase that served as the driving force behind the beautiful life and caring actions of 16-year-old Rebecca Kirtman. Becca, a Miami cheerleader, honor student and caring young woman, passed away in a tragic automobile accident on August 20, 2003. Today, her family and friends not only remember Becca for her great love and friendship, but also for her contributions to the community. Becca's Closet provides formal attire to high school students who otherwise would not be able to attend their prom/homecoming. Our mission is to continue her vision and dream of helping others. In Becca's memory, scholarships are awarded to deserving high school students to advance their education.

Care Bags Foundation

www.carebags4kids.org

Annie Wignall of Newton, IA is the founder and director of the Care Bags Foundation, an organization she started when she was eleven years old. Care Bags provides essential, fun, safe and age appropriate things (games, toothbrushes, books, etc.) to kids during difficult times in their lives. Care bags go to over 800 disadvantaged, abused and displaced kids every year. These bags are distributed by 20 agencies serving over 80 towns in Iowa as well as going to other states for disaster relief and to needy kids all over the world via Airline Ambassadors.

Using the Care Bags Starter Kit, other young people have adopted Annie's program and are implementing it in their own communities.

Carolyn's Compassionate Children

www.childrencc.com

Carolyn Rubenstein founded Carolyn's Compassionate Children in 1999 when she was 13 years old. Carolyn's Compassionate Children is a support organization linking critically ill children and children with life challenges to volunteer teens in schools through letter writing. The organization has since expanded to include organizing annual school supply, holiday letter, and gift drives and awarding college scholarships.

Chores-For-Charity

www.choresforcharity.com

Ilana Rothbein founded Chores-For-Charity as a way to raise money for FACES (Finding a Cure for Epilepsy and Seizures). Juggling schoolwork, sports, social activities and part-time work, she found it very difficult to organize a fundraiser. Instead, Ilana decided to donate the money from her babysitting jobs to FACES. Over a year, she donated 45 hours of her time babysitting and $450 of her earnings to FACES. She thought, "Maybe I can get other kids to do the same thing. Since kids are donating their time to contribute their earnings to a charitable organization, it's only fair that those hours be counted as charitable work." She began developing her personal fundraising project into an official program with support from her family and FACES.

Cody's Individual Comfort Kits

www.codyscomfortkits.com

A visit to the Emergency Department at Kemptville District Hospital prompted Cody to develop the idea for "Cody's Individual Comfort Kits." These individual kits are to be given to young patients to help make their visit to the hospital a more comfortable, less frightening experience. Following a fundraising drive in September 2002 Cody assembled the first comfort kits. The free kits, for children aged infant to 16, contain books, blankets, videos, toys, rattles, and other things to make a child's stay at hospital easier. Cody has already delivered over 200 Comfort Kits and has also created "Grandma and Grandpa Kits" for older patients staying in Kemptville District Hospital.

Free the Children

www.freethechildren.org

After reading an article about a 12 year-old Pakistani boy who was murdered for speaking out against child labor in his country, 12 year-old Craig Kielburger of Toronto, Canada decided to start an organization where kids could help increase awareness of child labor and child poverty around the world and take action to combat these problems. Free the Children has branches in over 35 countries.

Grandmas Gifts

www.grandmasgifts.org

Inspired by the memory of her grandmother who lived in Appalachian Ohio, 9 year-old Emily Douglas established a nonprofit organization called Grandmas Gifts. Since 1992, Emily has raised over half a million dollars worth of food, clothing, toys, books and educational field trips for schools, children, and organizations in the area. Emily hopes that Grandma's Gifts will raise awareness of economic hardship in the Appalachian Ohio region, bridge the cultural gap between Appalachia and the rest of the United States and show other young people how service to the community can be a fun and worthwhile endeavor.

Kids For A Clean Environment (F.A.C.E.)

www.kidsface.org

Kids F.A.C.E. is an international children's environmental organization started in 1989 by 9 year-old Melissa Poe of Nashville, TN. The club was established to provide a way for children to be involved in the protection of nature and connect them with other children who shared their concerns about global environmental issues. Kids F.A.C.E. currently has 300,000 members worldwide, and together they've planted over a million trees!

Kids Helping Kids

www.kidshelpingkids.org

In 1997, a year after being diagnosed with a brain tumor, Mischa Zimmermann established Kids Helping Kids. A nonprofit volunteer organization run by teens to benefit teens and children affected by catastrophic illness or injury. KHK provides support with peer interaction, mobility equipment and special wishes while also raising awareness of the life changes these individuals and their families face. The teens who are a part of KHK often help with event and activity planning, learning the value of contributing their time and developing a profound sense of commitment to something bigger than themselves.

Kids Konnected

www.kidskonnected.org

Jon Wagner-Holtz, an eleven year old boy, started Kids Konnected in 1993 after his mother was treated for breast cancer. Jon founded Kids Konnected because he couldn't find any programs that could help him find other kids to talk to who knew what it was like to have a sick parent. Kids Konnected started in California and now has programs across the United States. The organization offers a 24 hour hotline, an email newsletter, a chat room, monthly meetings, resources and summer camps.

Kids Saving the Rainforest

www.kidssavingtherainforest.org

When they were nine years old, Janine Licare Andrews and Aislin Livingstone sold painted rocks at a roadside table in Manuel Antonio, Costa Rica to raise money to help protect local rainforests and endangered wildlife. In 1999, the girls opened a store to sell their artwork as well as the work of local artists and craftspeople. All of the store's profits go toward preserving rainforest land, rehabilitating baby animals and educating people around the world about the connection between humans and nature.

Kids Who Care Foundation

www.kidswhocareclub.org

Risha, a 7 year-old who underwent an Auto Islet Cell Transplant for Chronic Pancreatitis in March 2004, understands very well the challenges of being in the hospital room and staring at the bare white walls! The Kids Who Care Foundation, a nonprofit organization, was founded by Risha to help and support other kids with Pancreatitis and other chronic diseases. Rishi's mission is to brighten the days at the hospital for kids that are having major surgeries. She does this by making cards with the help of friends and neighbors. She sends them cards with the hope of making them feel better and making their rooms cheerful from kids who care.

Project Linus

www.projectlinus.org

Project Linus is an organization dedicated to providing handmade blankets to babies, children suffering from serious illness and trauma as well as those in hospitals, cancer treatment facilities, clinics, hospices and homeless shelters. The site contains information about local Project Linus chapters and quilt patterns.

Ryan's Well Foundation

www.ryanswell.ca

At the age of six, Ryan Hrelijac learned that without access to clean water people become ill and sometimes even died. He set out to raise $70 towards building a well in Africa and, having reached his goal in four months, Ryan kept working and organizing. He has now raised over $1,000,000 and his work has helped to change the lives of thousands of people in Africa who might not otherwise have been able to lead healthy, normal lives. Ryan's Well Foundation has come together to continue this important and inspiring work.

Streaming Futures

www.kidzonline.org/streamingfutures

Streaming Futures is a free, web-based career program dedicated to helping teens choose the right career path by allowing them to watch internet-based video interviews with career professionals from a wide variety of fields. Founded by Joel Holland when he was 15, Streaming Futures received funding from Nortel Networks, the federal government and became part of the Nortel Networks Kidz Online content program. The online show is seen in thousands of high school classrooms across the country and continues to grow as Joel travels around the nation interviewing success stories in all types of careers.

Students for Organ Donation

www.studentdonor.org

Students for Organ Donation is a student-run, nonprofit organization dedicated to helping close the gap between the supply and demand for vital organs and tissue. Working within the framework of universities throughout the nation, Students for Organ Donation seeks to promote organ donation, awareness, and registration among students, staff, and members of the community.

Students Together for Autism Research (S.T.A.R.)

www.s-t-a-r.org

S.T.A.R. was founded in 2005 by Matthew Cortland and Tina Liu, both juniors at Cherokee High School in Marlton, NJ. This organization began as a small group raising money and walking at the Autism Walk, and now has burgeoned into Students Together for Autism Research! As co-founders of this organization, Matthew and Tina are determined to spread S.T.A.R. across the nation to raise student awareness about Autism. S.T.A.R. encourages student involvement to aid in raising Autism awareness through community service and fundraising and by creating S.T.A.R. clubs in schools across the country.

TakingITGlobal

www.takingitglobal.org

The TakingITGlobal Online Community sprung from a conversation between its two co-founders, Jennifer Corriero and Davie Furdyk, aged 19 and 17 at the time, who were striving to use technology to improve education and opportunities for youth around the world. Jennifer and Davie wanted to share their business and leadership experiences with other youth and provide them with empowering, meaningful experiences. As young tech-savvy leaders, they were able to make their visions a reality with the help of a core team of volunteers equally dedicated to the mission of TIG. The source of energy and imagination behind TakingITGlobal continues to grow with innovation, an entrepreneurial spirit, and a desire to make positive change in the world.

Teen Force

www.teenforce.net

Brynn MacDonald founded Teen Force after a teen advice site, she volunteered with, shut down. Brynn is dedicated to building Teen Force into the best worldwide outreach program for teens. The website offers one-on-one, teen-to-teen advice as well as online teen programs, teen-written articles, and a place for teens to share their stories.

The Cello Cries On

http:members.sigecom.net/jdc

Jason Crowe started the Cello Cries On in 1998 in the wake of the mortar attack on civilians standing in a Sarajevo market during the war in Bosnia-Hercegovina. The attack killed 22 people. Jason was ten years old when he started the Cello Cries On, named in honor of Vedran Smailovic, a cellist in the Sarajevo Opera Orchestra who visited the market the day after the attack and proceeded to play his cello in the market for 22 days in memory of the people who died in the attack. The main project of the Cello Cries On is to raise money for the creation of a statue that will be given to the citizens of Bosnia-Hercegovina from kids around the world in the name of peace and harmony. Jason also publishes The Informer, a newspaper for kids that has readers in 29 states and 15 countries.

The Victorian Hands Foundation

www.tvhf.org

Nadia Campbell founded the Victorian Hands Foundation when she was 18 in memory of her late aunt, Victoria. After watching a television special on elder abuse, she wanted to help the seniors in her community. Through the organization, youth volunteers work to make seniors feel loved and appreciated through programs like "Adopt a Grandparent."

Unite for Sight

www.uniteforsight.org

Unite For Sight, an organization founded in 2000 by 18 year-old Jennifer Staple, is dedicated to preventing blindness through free community vision screenings, public education about eye disease and the importance of regular eye exams to prevent blindness, a speaker series and an eyeglass drive. Vision screening and vision education programs are conducted at local community centers, including schools, soup kitchens, and libraries. Unite for Sight is also committed to supporting those community members with deteriorating vision through community assistance.

Youth Action International and PeaceForKids.Org

www.peaceforkids.org

Youth Action International and PeaceForKids.Org were founded by Kimmie Weeks to give young people a chance to participate in pressing humanitarian problems around the world. Since its establishment, Youth Action International has raised thousands of dollars for humanitarian programs and Kimmie Weeks has been a huge activist for child soldiers and an inspiration to U.S. children. Kimmie has been working on projects for peace since he was 11 years old.

Youth for a Better World

www.angelfire.com/home/ymbw

Lindsay Logsdon of Amherstburg, Ontario, Canada started Youth for a Better World with her sister Brittany in September 2000 because they wanted to help solve problems they saw around the world. Youth for a Better World has organized fundraisers for the local battered women's shelter and a food bank and collected toys to send to a children's hospital in East Timor. They also sponsor a child through World Vision Canada.

Youth for Environmental Sanity—YES!

www.yesworld.org

Youth for Environmental Sanity was founded in 1990 by 16 year-old Ocean Robbins and 19 year-old Ryan Eliason to educate, inspire, and empower youth to join forces for social justice and environmental sanity. Since 1990, YES! has spoken in person to 620,000 students in school assemblies, held 83 week-long youth action training camps and hundreds of day-long workshops and inspired the formation of more than 400 nonprofit clubs and organizations working for positive change. YES! supports youth committed to building a just and sustainable world, helping young change makers to expand effectiveness, network with one another, and gain the support they'll need for a lifetime of action. YES! alumni have persuaded schools and businesses to purchase recycled products, offer organic and vegetarian options in cafeterias, retrofit their lighting and offer anti-prejudice trainings.

25 Top Children's Charities

According to the National Center for Charitable Statistics, the United States had 902,270 public charities in 2006. You can choose to give your money to help build houses for the poor, find cures for diseases, protect endangered animals or help children learn to read. The problem isn't finding a charity to support, but narrowing down your options and choosing the one that suits you.

1.   Advancement Via Individual Determination Center

AVID is an educational program that helps C and D students improve their chances of getting into college. Students, most of whom are underprivileged, can begin the program as early as the fourth grade. They work with specially trained teachers and tutors to learn organizational and study skills and develop critical thinking abilities. Ninety-five percent of AVID graduates go to college, and 85% remain enrolled in college after two years. AVID is active in 1,500 schools in 21 states and 15 countries. For more information, visit **www.avidonline.org.**

2.   Big Brothers Big Sisters of America

Big Brothers Big Sisters of America (BBSSA) is the oldest and largest youth mentoring organization in the United States. They serve over 220,000 six- to 18-year-old kids, with a goal of reaching one million by 2010. BBBSA mentors work one-on-one with children, helping them improve their study habits, develop confidence, and learn to relate to adults. The relationship they mentor and child develop has a direct and measurable impact on the child's life: children in the BBSSA program are less likely to use drugs, use illegal alcohol, and skip school. They also do better in their schoolwork and get along better with their families. For more information about BBSSA, go to **www.bbbsa.org.**

3.   Boys & Girls Clubs of America

Boys & Girls Clubs of America began in 1860 when several women in Hartford, Conn. decided to develop a positive alternative for boys who were roaming the streets. Originally called the Boys Club, girls were added to the program in 1990, and girls now make up 45% of the membership. Now, Boys and Girls Clubs of America has around 4,300 clubs in all 50 states, Puerto Rico, the Virgin Islands, and on U.S. military bases around the world. 4.8 million boys and girls are served by the more than 50,000 trained professional staff members and volunteers who work for the organization. The Boys & Girls Club is a neighborhood-based building, often a school, that offers youth programs and activities every day, after school and on weekends. Through the Club, children have a safe place to hang out, learn, and grow.

For more information about Boys and Girls Clubs of America, go to **www.bgca.org.**

4.   Campaign for Tobacco-Free Kids

Tobacco use is the leading preventable cause of death in the United States. Nearly 23 percent of high school students smoke, with 1,500 more kids becoming daily smokers every day. The Campaign for Tobacco-Free Kids goals are to prevent kids from smoking, help smokers quit and protect people from secondhand smoke. Some specific initiatives they are working toward include pushing for higher cigarette taxes and legislation to give the FDA authority over tobacco products and marketing.

Go to **www.tobaccofreekids.org** for more information about the Campaign for Tobacco-Free Kids.

5.   Canines for Disabled Kids

Canines for Disabled Kids (CDK) began in 1998. This organization provides assistance dogs to children under age 12 who are autistic or have hearing or physical disabilities. Since its inception, CDK has placed sponsored over 90 assistance dogs. In addition to helping with the daily tasks of life, these assistance dogs provide companionship to the children and help them develop confidence and responsibility.

For more information about CDK, go to **www.caninesforkids.org.**

6. CASA

CASA, or Court-Appointed Special Advocates, began in Seattle in 1977 when a judge began using trained community volunteers to speak for the best interests of abused and neglected children in court. CASA now has 59,000 volunteers in over 900 areas and serves 243,000 abused and neglected children.

CASA volunteers are appointed by judges and act as officers of the court. Their duty is to research the background of an assigned case, speak on behalf of the child in the courtroom and to represent the child's best interests throughout the case – which may last for as long as two years.

For more information about CASA, visit **www.nationalcasa.org.**

7. Children's Defense Fund

The Children's Defense Fund (CDF) has a mission to ensure that every child has a *Healthy Start*, a *Head Start*, a *Fair Start*, a *Safe Start*, and a *Moral Start* in life and successful passage to adulthood with the help of caring families and communities. Specific programs they focus on include children's health insurance, summer and after-school enrichment programs, scholarships and leadership development.

See **www.childrensdefense.org** for more information about the Children's Defense Fund.

8.   Communities in Schools

Communities in Schools (CIS) is a dropout prevention program that connects community resources with student needs. Specific services this group offers include mentoring, counseling, vision screening, day care, job training, and gang prevention. CIS operates at 2,500 schools in 32 states, reaching 1.9 million kids annually.

For more information about CIS, visit **www.cisnet.org.**

9.   International Child Art Foundation

The International Child Art Foundation (ICAF) fosters children's creativity by sponsoring art programs, exhibitions, and festivals for children and of children's artwork. They also have a healing arts program that uses art to help children recover from disasters. For more information, visit **www.icaf.org.**

10.   KaBOOM!

Since 1995, KaBOOM! has helped build more than 400 playgrounds, skate parks, ice rinks, and athletic fields in low-income areas around the United States. They have also helped renovate thousands of other play areas and provide training and expertise for communities that want to build their own playgrounds. They were instrumental in building 100 new playgrounds along the Gulf Coast after Hurricanes Katrina and Rita struck that area. For more information about KaBOOM!, visit **www.kaboom.org.**

11.   Locks of Love

Locks of Love uses real, donated hair to make high-quality hairpieces for children who have suffered hair loss due to medical conditions. Their mission is to return a sense of self-confidence and normalcy to these children. The hairpieces are provided free of charge or on a sliding scale, depending on the financial need of the recipient. More than 2,000 children in all 50 states and Canada have been helped by Locks of Love.

For more information about Locks of Love, go to **www.locksoflove.org.**

12.   Make-a-Wish Foundation

The Make-a-Wish Foundation is the world's largest wish-granting organization. In 2007, they granted wishes to 13,006 children suffering from life-threatening medical conditions. Since its beginning in 1980, this organization has granted more than 165,000 wishes. From an afternoon spent as a police officer or fire fighter to a visit to Disney World, the 25,000 volunteers who are part of the Make-A-Wish Foundation give ill children their greatest wishes.

To learn how you can donate to the Make-a-Wish Foundation, visit **www.wish.org.**

13.   March of Dimes

March of Dimes is an organization dedicated to improving the health of babies by preventing birth defects, premature birth, and infant mortality. Founded in 1938 as the National Foundation for Infantile Paralysis, the original mission of the March of Dimes was to find a vaccine for polio and to care for polio victims. Since that initial success, it has also been instrumental in developing newborn screening tests, identifying healthy habits for pregnant women, pioneering fetal surgical techniques, and working to reduce premature births. The name "March of Dimes" was coined because of an initial campaign that requested donors send dimes to help fund polio research. The name was officially changed in 1979.One of the major fundraisers sponsored by the March of Dimes is the annual Walk America, which has helped raise more than $1.7 billion since its inception in 1970.For more information about the March of Dimes, visit **www.marchofdimes.com.**

14.   My Stuff Bags Foundation

Over 300,000 abused, abandoned, and neglected children across America are removed from dangerous home environments each year. They often arrive at crisis centers and foster homes with few, if any, personal belongings. The My Stuff Bags Foundation seeks to give these children comfort and hope by providing them with a My Stuff Bag full of things they need to help them settle in their new environments, such as clothes, toys, toiletries, stuffed animals, and a security blanket. My Stuff Bags has provided bags to more than 320,000 children in 49 states since it began in 1998. Their goal is to have a bag for every child removed from his or her home. For more information, go to **www.mystuffbags.org.**

15. National Center for Missing and Exploited Children

Since its beginning in 1984, the National Center for Missing and Exploited Children (NCMEC) has sought to prevent child abduction and sexual exploitation, find missing children, help victims of child abduction and sexual exploitation, as well as their families. Some specific programs the NCMEC conduct include serving as a clearinghouse for information about missing and exploited children, distributing photographs and descriptions of missing children and operating a hotline for reporting Internet-related child sexual exploitation. NCMEC also assists and trains law enforcement agencies and social service professionals to prevent, investigate, prosecute and treat cases involving missing and exploited children

For more information about NCMEC, visit **www.missingkids.com.**

16. North American Council on Adoptable Children

The North American Council on Adoptable Children (NACAC) helps find permanent, loving homes for children once considered unadoptable or hard to place. They may be school-aged children, many of whom have physical, mental, or emotional difficulties. They also help adults through the pre-adoption process and provide support to adoptive families.

For more information about NACAC, go to **www.nacac.org.**

17. Partnership for a Drug-Free America

The Partnership for a Drug-Free America unites parents, scientists, and communicators to help families raise healthy children. It offers research-based public education programs that help parents to keep their children from using drugs and alcohol and to find treatment for children who are in trouble.

For more information about the Partnership for a Drug-Free America, visit http://www.drugfree.org.

18.   Ronald McDonald House Charities

Ronald McDonald House Charities (RMHC) seeks to create, find, and support programs that directly improve the health and well-being of children. They are probably most well known for their Ronald McDonald houses that provide a home away from home for families of seriously ill children receiving treatment at nearby hospitals. However, RMHC also has other programs.   A Ronald McDonald Family Room located near the pediatric areas of many hospitals. This room provides parents of children in the hospital a comfortable place to sit and relax.   Ronald McDonald Care Mobiles that bring medical, dental and health education services to underserved children around the world. Grants to help other not-for-profit organizations that serve children worldwide. Scholarships to students entering college across the United States.

For more information, visit **www.rmhc.org.**

19.   Reach Out and Read

Children who are read to during the first years of life are more likely to learn to read on schedule, priming them for success in school and throughout life. Through Reach Out and Read (ROR), pediatricians, family physicians, and nurses make reading a part of pediatric primary care. At well-child check-ups, they encourage parents to read aloud to their children and give each child between the ages of six months and five years a new children's book to keep. More than 14,000 pediatricians participate in ROR throughout all 50 states, the District of

Columbia, Puerto Rico, and Guam. In 2007, they distributed 4.6 million books to 2.8 million U.S. infants, toddlers, and preschoolers.

For more information, visit **www.reachoutandread.org.**

20.   Save the Children

The original Save the Children Fund began in England in 1919 and provided aid to children in Vienna affected by World War I. It was reborn in the United States in 1932 as an organization designed to help the people of Appalachia who were struggling through the Great Depression. Since then, Save the Children has grown to a worldwide organization serving 37 million children in more than 50 countries. Programs include food aid, education, health care, and economic-development programs. While Save the Children may be best known for its child sponsorship programs around the world, it has several active programs in the United States, including; After-school programs for more than 125,000 children, Eye care services and glasses to Navajo and Hopi children in New Mexico and Arizona. A Family Day Care Network that trains women to start in-home child care centers and offers referrals to parents seeking child care

For more information, go to **www.savethechildren.org.**

Beth Rosenthal Davis

21. Shriner's Hospitals for Children

Shriner's Hospitals for Children is an international health care system of 22 hospitals that provide care for children up to the age of 18 who have orthopedic conditions, burns, spinal cord injuries, and cleft lip and palate. The children are cared for in a family-centered environment at no charge, regardless of financial need. The first Shriner's Hospital began in 1919 and was founded by the Shriner's of North America. It is still supported by donations from the Shriner's fraternity and from the public. For more information, visit **www.shrinershq.org.**

22. Special Olympics

Special Olympics offers year-round training and competition in 30 Olympic-type sports to children and adults who have intellectual disabilities. They help participants improve their physical fitness and motor skills, develop greater self-confidence and a more positive self-image, discover new talents and abilities, make new friends, and become productive and respected members of society. Special Olympics serves 2.5 million people in over 180 countries. For more information, go to **www.specialolympics.org.**

23.   St. Jude Children's Research Hospital

St. Jude is a hospital located in Memphis, Tennessee that treats children with serious illnesses such as cancer, AIDS, and sickle cell anemia. In addition to the hospital, St. Jude also includes a research facility dedicated to raising the survival rate for many diseases. Because of research done at St. Jude, the survival rate for some pediatric cancers has increased from 20 to 70 percent. Founded in 1962 by actor Danny Thomas, children from all 50 states and around the world have been treated at St. Jude. All told, St. Jude's treats some 4,300 children a year — at no cost to their families. It is the third largest health care charity in the United States and has more than one million volunteers nationwide. The primary funding arm for St. Jude is the American Lebanese Syrian Associated Charities. For more information about St. Jude, visit **www.stjude.org.**

24.   Toys for Tots

Toys for Tots is a mission of the U.S. Marine Corps Reserve. During October, November and December each year, Toys for Tots volunteers collect new, unwrapped toys in their community and distribute them as Christmas gifts to needy children in that same community. Toys for Tots began in 1947 when Marine Reservists in Los Angeles collected and distributed 5,000 toys to needy children. The organization grew and spread to other communities, and in 2006, local Toys for Tots Coordinators distributed 19.2 million toys to 7.6 million needy children in 558 communities throughout all 50 states, the District of Columbia, Puerto Rico, and the Virgin Islands. All told, the Toys for Tots program has distributed more than 370 million toys to more than 173 million needy children. For more information about Toys for Tots, including how to volunteer or to donate money or toys, visit **www.toysfortots.org.**

25.   United States Fund for UNICEF

UNICEF began after World War II to supply milk and food to starving children in Europe, the Middle East, and China. Today, UNICEF is active in more than 150 countries and territories around the world, helping to develop community-based programs to promote health and immunization programs, basic education, nutrition, safe water supply and sanitation services, and emergency relief.   The United States Fund for UNICEF supports the worldwide UNICEF program and focuses on five major priorities: education,   emergencies,   HIV/AIDS, immunization, and malnutrition. For more information, see www.unicefusa.org.

Books On Teaching Kids To Care

The BIG HELP : THE BIG HELP (Nickelodeon)by Alan Goodman, illustrated by Fiona Smyth. New York: Pocket Books, 1994.

The Difference a Day Makes : 365 Ways to Change Your World in Just 24 Hoursby Karen M. Jones.

How to Make the World a Better Place: 116 Ways You Can Make a Differenceby Jeffrey Hollender, Linda Catling.

The Littlest Volunteers,published by the Oranges and Short Hills, New Jersey, and written by League member Danielle Speckhart, is a story that is dedicated to all children who have a big heart. the book inspires all of us, even young children, to help build better communities.

What Kids Need to Succeed: Proven, Practical Ways to Raise Good Kids by Peter L. Benson, Judy Galbraith and Pamela Espeland. Minneapolis, MN: Free Spirit Publishing, 1998.This book is based on a nationwide survey of 100,000 young people in over 200 communities. It teaches about the need for family support, strong community values, service to others, and more than 30 additional other keys for success.

What Would We Do Without You?: A Guide to Volunteer Activities for Kids by Kathy Henderson. White Hall, VA: Betterway Publications, 1990.This book identifies volunteer service that young people have provided and describes ways to be involved and be a good volunteer.

The Social Cause Diet by Gail Perry Johnston. Lafayette, CA: Cupola Press, 2008 This book claims that our country doesn't need another program for losing weight, but we could use a plan for losing a little of ourselves. We could all benefit from going on the Social Cause Diet: a diet that involves intentionally giving of ourselves to others in service.

Building Bridges: Connecting Classroom and Community through Service-Learning in Social Studies (Bulletin (National Council for the Social Studies), No 97) by Rahima C. Wade. Washington, DC: National Council for the Social Studies, 2000.

Do Something in Your City (Do Something About It) by Amanda Rondeau.Edina, MN: ABDO, 2004.

AMAZING KIDS (Kidbacks) by Paula N. Kessler and illustrated by J.J. Smith-Moore. New York: Random House, 1995.

Web Resources

Articles on Volunteering – from the Boston Parents' Paper
http://topics-az.parenthood.com/subcategory/Volunteer.html
Links to articles about families and volunteering, ranging from ways to become more involved in schools, ways to scale down for the holidays, etc.

http://blossominternational.org/: Blossom International is a site for children to volunteer. They encourage them to become proactive, empowered and engaged members of their communities.

http://leagueworldwide.org/: The LEAGUE combines service, learning, and friendly "co-opetition" with live, interactive events. From planting trees to collecting food for the hungry, kids are returning millions of dollars' worth of value back to the community.

http://www.monterey.org/: The Volunteer program is designed for young people of many skills and interests. As a Volunteer, you will have the opportunity to contribute your unique talents and energy toward the growth of the Monterey community.

http://coastalpetrescue.org/: The teens will work with adult volunteers of the organization in helping pets get adopted, organizing fundraisers, and even planning community events.

http://www.kidscanmakeadifference.org/: KIDS is an innovative educational program for middle- and high-school students. It helps them understand the root causes of hunger and poverty and how they-as individuals-can take action.

http://www.geocities.com/volguide/: This site is just a guide for teens. To help them get started in volunteer work.

http://www.newglobalcitizens.org/: New Global Citizens educates, equips and mobilizes young people to help solve the greatest challenges faced by communities around the world by partnering with grassroots organizations that are finding local solutions to local problems.

Activities To Instill A Sense Of Empathy In Children
Mentioned Throughout This Book

- School-aged children may enjoy visiting nursing home residents who may not have many guests. Contact the Recreation Director at a nearby facility to ask whether there are any residents who would enjoy the company. Playing board games together, working on puzzles or even simply chatting can brighten the day of a lonely man or woman. Kids who play musical instruments can volunteer to share their music with the elderly.

- Establish a relationship with your neighbors, bake brownies to welcome new ones

- Plant produce and donate the harvest to a local food bank.

- Plant seeds. Sell the flowers or plants and donate the proceeds to a local homeless shelters.

- Pick up litter at a park.

- Make treats or draw pictures for a local senior home.

- Pick up trash on the school grounds.

- Develop and maintain a recycling program at school.

- Collect food, warm clothing, toys, or personal care items for the needy. Deliver to shelters. *Remember shelters are in need of supplies all year long!*

- Hold a Teddy Bear and Friends (Stuffed Animals) Drive. Donate the collected animals to a Homeless Shelter for new arrivals.

- Encourage friends to donate gently used books to families in shelters, low income preschools or hospitals.

- Donate video tapes, DVD's, or unused video games to local pediatric hospitals or shelters.

- Collect unused make-up, perfume and other cosmetics for a center for abused women.

- Hold a drive to collect baby items and donate to teen moms in alternative schools.

- Make center pieces, holiday cards, birthday cards, and notes for assisted living facilities, children hospital wards, or meals on wheels.

- Make Halloween bags of candy for homeless kids Be sure all candy is individually wrapped and avoid candy with peanuts.

- Have a drive to collect NEW socks and underwear for foster kids

- Donate used eye glasses to an organization or place that recycles them for the needy.

- Collect gently used stuffed animals and dolls, clean them up, repair and donate them.

- Collect gently used clothes and donate them for a dress-up area at a daycare or family shelter.

- Make a holiday basket for someone in need.

- Serve a meal at a homeless shelter

- Write letters or draw pictures to service men/women. Fill shoe boxes with candy and snack to send troops.

- Have friends and family members collect travel sized hotel toiletries

- donate to homeless shelters

- make welcome cards to make the residents feel welcome to their new "home"

- Put together a care-package for service men/women.

- Put together a care-package for teen moms.

- Form a litter patrol on school or park ground.

- In December, contact a tree farm or nursery about donating a Christmas tree to a needy family, shelter or nursing home, or buy a tree to donate

- Hold a food drive to help keep food bank shelves well stocked

- Donate gift cards for teens in foster care, they are the most forgotten.

- Ask your friends to donate $5 grocery gift cards each time they go to the grocery store for their family. Put all the cards together and provide a complete Thanksgiving meal for a family who may be down on their luck.

- Offer to walk a neighbors pet if they are feeling ill.

- Make cookies for a new family in the neighborhood.

- Write a compliment and give it so someone who did something nice.

- Have your child pick out school supplies for someone who needs them at back to school time.

- Have an UN-birthday party at a shelter and bring ice cream, cake and a gift for each child there.

- Cut down on holiday gift giving and give a gift to someone who really needs one.

- Keep non-perishable food in the car at all times in case you see someone who is hungry.

- Donate diapers to low income childcare centers, homeless or domestic violence shelters.

- Grow your hair and your child's too. When it reaches a really long length, cut off 11 inches and send it to Locks Of Love to have a wig made for a sick child who has no hair. Your hair will grow back, theirs may not.

- Hold a penny drive. People don't mind getting rid of them and they add up.

- Keep an empty 5 gallon water bottle in your house. Drop your pocket change in it at the end of the day. When it is full have your family decide how to spend the money.

- Have a bake sale or set up a lemonade stand and donate the money to charity.

- After your child's birthday party ask them to choose one of the gifts to give to someone else. Birthday and holiday time is also a great time to have your child choose toys to give away to someone else to make room for their new ones.

- Cut back on holiday spending. Sometimes less is more. In some countries, kids get pennies in their shoes.

- Donate clothing when no longer used. Donate unused toys too.

- Special Olympics- Volunteer at the next Special Olympics event in your area. specialolympics.org.

- Help the animals. Children love animals, so why not use this interest to help out at your local Humane Society by donating your time or supplies (pet food, old blankets).

- Plan a charity carnival for your backyard complete with carnival games, refreshments, and prizes. Afterwards, donate all the proceeds to your favorite charity. Invite friends from your neighborhood, place of worship, and your children's classes by printing up flyers (indicating which charity will benefit). Charge a set fee for entrance. You can set up a ticket booth and give guests tickets to use for games and refreshments.

- **Support a Local United Way Charity.** Use the United Way website to find a volunteer opportunity in your neighborhood.

- For many kids, Halloween is one of the most fun holidays of the year. What could be better than getting dressed up in a crazy costume and going from door to door to get tons of free candy? Your family can have fun on Halloween and at the same time help children and families in need Donating your candy, collecting change for UNICEF

- Hold a car wash

- Hold a community garage sale and raise money for charity

- Hold a bake sale

- Donate used board games, video games, movies and other toys your kids no longer use to local shelters

- Donate the books your child has outgrown

- Collect recipes from friends and family members and make a cookbook. Sell it to raise money for charity.

- Encourage families at your child's school to make pans of pasta and salad. Sell tickets to a spaghetti dinner and donate the money to charity.

- Go to garage sales. Buy **new** toys and clothing and donate them to kids who need them. You can use the money from your family charity box to buy the goods. "Garage saling" is a fun thing to do together.

- Older kids can tutor low income children needing help in school.

- Have a movie night, charge admission and provide snacks. Donate the money to charity.

- Older children who babysit can offer to babysit for free for single parents who need a night out.

- Volunteer to set up a gift wrap station at holiday time. Gift wrap at no charge and encourage customers to give a donation.

- Donate Halloween candy. Excess candy can be donated to Meals on Wheels, nursing or veterans' homes, shelters or agencies that work with children (such as foster care, group, or transition homes). Treats like these are especially appreciated on Veterans' Day, Thanksgiving and other holiday parties.

- Save coupons and give them to people who need them.

- Knit hats for people with cancer

- Read to kids or do art projects at a shelter.

- Cut back on birthday gifts that your children don't need. Get them a few things and ask some (or all) guests to bring a gift for an underprivileged child or ask them to make a donation to charity.

- Serve a meal at a homeless shelter

- Write letters or draw pictures to service men/women. Fill shoe boxes with candy and snacks to send to the troops.

- Volunteer to take family photos at a homeless shelter. Print the photos and give them to the families. Many of them may have NO photos of their children.

- Make gifts for soldier serving our country.

About The Author

Beth Davis, lives in Miami with her husband Andy, daughter Rebekah, and son Benjamin. She is a National Board Certified Teacher who taught Elementary School for 17 years. Davis holds a Bachelor's Degree in Elementary Education from Florida International University, a Master's Degree in TESOL (Teaching Speakers of Other Languages) from Nova University, and an Education Specialist Degree in Computer Education from Barry University.

In 2005 she opened Kids For Kids Academy Preschool where she teaches families the school principles mentioned in this book. She also teaches preschoolers science in the school science lab. Davis' is also the author of **Hands On Minds On Preschool: A Blueprint To The World of Science and Math For Young Children**. (www.handsonmindsonpreschool.com) Beth Davis has written curriculum, books for teachers, lead teacher trainings, and has served on expert panels for the Florida Department of Education. She has also taught at Barry University.

She is the founder of Kids 4 Kids, Inc. a non-profit organization that teaches children to change the world through their acts of kindness. Since 1996, Kids 4 Kids has provided backpacks filled with school supplies and books for over 85,000 underprivileged children.

32335535R00103

Made in the USA
Charleston, SC
15 August 2014